A Wrestling Life

A Wrestling Life

The Inspiring Stories of Dan Gable

DAN GABLE

with SCOTT SCHULTE

UNIVERSITY OF IOWA PRESS *Iowa City*

University of Iowa Press, Iowa City 52242
Copyright © 2015 by the University of Iowa Press
www.uiowapress.org
Printed in the United States of America

Design by Richard Hendel

The stories in the book are based on the authors' memories
and interviews with relevant parties. The information within
is accurate to the best of the authors' knowledge and research.
Apologies in advance for any errors or omissions.

The University of Iowa Press is a member of Green Press Initiative
and is committed to preserving natural resources.

Printed on acid-free paper

ISBN: 978-1-60938-340-4 (cl)
ISBN: 978-1-60938-326-8 (pbk)
ISBN: 978-1-60938-330-5 (ebk)

Library of Congress Cataloging-in-Publication Data is on file
at the Library of Congress.

To the family I was born into—
my dad, Mack; my mom, Katie; and my sister, Diane—
all deceased, but still with me.
To the family that my wife and I helped create—
my wife, Kathy; daughter 1, Jenni; her husband,
Brian Mitchell; grandson 1, Gable; grandson 3, Jake;
granddaughter 2, Eliza; daughter 2, Annie; her husband,
Mike Gavin; grandson 2, Danny; granddaughter 1, Elsie;
granddaughter 3, Betsy; grandson 6, Archie; daughter 3, Molly;
her husband, Danny Olszta; grandson 4, Mickey; grandson 5,
Louie; grandson 7, Sammy; daughter 4, Mackenzie; and her
husband, Justin McCord.

To all future grandchildren and so on.

And to the family of wrestling!

—*Dan Gable*

For my father and mother who always believed in me.

—*Scott Schulte*

CONTENTS

ACKNOWLEDGMENTS

Beyond my family, the credit for where I am today goes to many that have contributed to my overall philosophy, which is still changing depending on what's better, updated, and working well:

It started with the YMCA in Waterloo, Iowa; then moved to my eighth grade algebra teacher and West Junior High wrestling coach, Martin Lundvall; then on to West High School and its famous wrestling coach and guidance counselor, Bob Siddens; on to Harold Nichols and Les Anderson, Iowa State University's national champion wrestling coaches; and then my last coaches at the Olympic level: Doug Blubaugh, Bill Farrell, Jim Peckham, and Bill Weick.

Moving on to my profession of wrestling coach, Coach Gary Kurdelmeier, Athletic Director Bump Elliott, and booster Roy Carver groomed me well.

All along the way, I always had strong friendships around me to cover my back and help me out when needed. One especially, Bob Altmaier, always kept me entertained and helped get my athletes into peak form. Mark Olinyk, thank you for easing tension on and off the mat.

Assisting along the way to make things happen when they needed to happen, Brett Mangold and Helen Hohle and Judy Leonard. It was a tough office to handle, but Assistant Coaches J Robinson and Mark Johnson made it easier for all.

The Hawkeye Wrestling Club and its board members all deserve thanks, especially Tom Senneff. The infamous Regina track coach Bob Brown, as well as Dave Culver, have my gratitude.

Flo Wrestling and CPOW for bringing wrestling to new levels of expertise. And ASICS for providing so much for the sport of wrestling.

And many thanks to a whole group of people who have been greatly significant to my life: David Gould, Tom Kenney, Tim Anderson,

ACKNOWLEDGMENTS

Frank Gifford, Eric Heneghan, Tim Johnson, Keith Knight, Doug Erwin, Dan McGivern, Nolan Zavoral, Russ Smith, and Pat McGrath.

To my early idols in wrestling: Bob Buzzard from East Waterloo and Tom Peckham from Cresco, Iowa, and to the Russians for giving me inspiration, knowledge, and toughness—thank you!

Thanks to all of my training partners over the years, especially Doug Moses, Dave Pruzansky, Bob Fouts, John Bowlsby, John and Ben Peterson, and even those who weren't wrestlers but lined up to alternate on me to help with my pre-Olympic workouts: Duane Benedict, Jack "Tito" Jones, and Dale Schroeder. The younger wrestlers, Tony Cordes, Randy Bensing, and others, whom I would wrestle two or three at a time, deserve mention. Some of my late-night workout partners at ISU, especially Chuck Jean, Norm Wilkerson, and Larry Munger, with whom I still fish, helped me a great deal.

My roommates in college at ISU, Dave Martin, Dave Bock, and Bill Krum, are all champion wrestlers and great people. The same is true of my roommates at the University of Iowa before I got married, Jon Marks, J. Robinson, Mike Narey, Joe Wells, and Matt Clarke.

And last, but certainly not least, I am grateful for all the Sunday late afternoon and evening gatherings at my parents' Waterloo home with my dad's friends, especially Jim Cordes and Gordy Moser, while I was at ISU. They would often call the coaches of wrestlers that I would be up against in the coming week and tell them to get ready, for I was coming to town. Thank God I was well prepared and, most of the time, ready!

Realizing I could write chapters on a whole lot more people just as deserving leads me to mention just a few more to close—Randy Lewis (most exciting), Bruce Kinseth (hardest worker), Chris Campbell (most talented), Royce Alger (toughest), Mark Mysnyk (most dedicated), Jessie Whitmer (strongest), Mark Ironside (most intense), Rico and Brinzer (fan favorites)...brothers, story after story. Stories to share in another book, with so many winners on and off the mat.

And finally, Mike Duroe, Pablo Ubasa, Fred Mims, Mike Doughty, Jed Brown, Bob Buckley, Mike Chapman, and Kyle Klingman. Thank you.

Dan Gable

To the Dan and Kathy Gable Family: thanks for allowing me into your lives.

To Dad and Mom: you taught me how to write and tell stories, and you even have learned to love wrestling. Okay, maybe not love, but you did allow me to let it become a major part of my life at a very young age. You never wavered in your support of my talent as a writer, and you always loved me. To Aaron Secrist: a great story of wrestling. Our friendship came out of our sons competing against each other at rival junior high schools. Had it not been for Aaron, I would not have attended the 2012 US Olympic Wrestling Trials, where this book first began. Thanks, Aaron. To Charlie Phillips: one of my closest friends and a great proofreader. Who would have thought those English classes back in 1982 would lead to this project? There are few finer men than Charlie Phillips. To Cindy Boyton: a great writer and friend, you have always been my mentor and a great coach. This book was made possible in large part due to Cindy's constant pushing. Thanks, C! To Guy Yocum: an editor at *Golf Digest*, it was you, Guy, who gave me the ultimate pep talk on that one Saturday night in 2013. No sugarcoating, and I thank you for seeing the potential and not allowing me to squander it away. To Luke and Allison Lofthouse: thanks for being my taxi service during my times in Iowa City.

To my family: Taylor and Krista and my grandchildren and Elder Doug Schulte. In your own unique ways, you encouraged me to succeed. I love you.

Scott Schulte

INTRODUCTION

Dan Gable

A writer named Scott Schulte approached me recently and started a conversation. He caught me in an emotional state, just as the Hawkeyes' last chance to make the Olympic freestyle team was lost when Brent Metcalf dropped a match by a criteria tiebreaker. It was especially tough because 75 percent of the sold-out crowd that day were Iowa fans and thought Metcalf had actually won, only to be disappointed by the result.

While it was already an emotional moment, Scott brought up the possibility of doing an article for an Internet media outlet about another very difficult subject from my personal life, my sister's murder when I was a teenager. I agreed, and as that project developed, Scott suggested we do a book of "Gable short stories." Having many such stories from over the years, I thought it was a good idea, but I figured it would only end up being all talk and that nothing would come of it.

But before long, we were actually getting work done. Since Scott lived in Connecticut at the time of putting this book together, I was able to learn to be more tech-active, which is a good thing (I think). So I am now officially more educated and can hopefully bring my message to the masses in more positive ways.

So here we are . . . enjoy! I still have many more stories that are worthwhile, enjoyable, and educational, so if this goes well, maybe you can look for a second book, since there is so much that we had to leave out! Besides, I'm still creating stories, because my work is never done.

INTRODUCTION
Scott Schulte

I've made a career out of telling stories. On most occasions they are stories I enjoy telling. I get to meet interesting people and convey their experiences. The stories I tell have landed on the pages of newspapers and magazines, and I have always said, "What a great job I have!"

Through such experiences, I developed an idea for a different kind of biographical book, much like the one you are reading now. As I imagined it, each chapter was going to be a stand-alone story from the person's life, a kind of snapshot or highlight. This way, you could get the chance to read the exciting or important parts of a person's life without all of the extra, and sometimes unnecessary, details.

After hashing out the details of how I would create such a book, I was faced with the challenge of finding a person I found interesting and whose name was big enough to carry a full book of stories.

Then I went to the 2012 US Olympic Wrestling Trials.

We all have childhood heroes. For me, there were many individuals who stood out in my young mind. No one was more important than my father and mother. Even as a young person and teenager, they were my heroes. But the athlete I admired most was the great Dan Gable. I was a wrestler, and as someone who graduated from high school in 1982, wrestling began and ended with Gable. Everything I heard in practice or at camps and clinics would always somehow include a story of him. If I did not have posters and cutouts from magazines of the legend, I might not have believed that he actually existed. I would have just figured he was some mythic figure.

Growing up, I was at a few clinics where Gable instructed. I never approached him, but I was once used as the practice "dummy" as he instructed a move. The move hurt, but I didn't care. I was hanging out with Dan Gable!

When I served my Mormon mission to Los Angeles, the 1984 Olympics were held there, and I was fortunate to see the freestyle wrestling competition. Coaching the team was none other than Dan Gable.

When the opportunity came to actually meet Gable at the 2012 Olympic Trials in Iowa City, I took it. My initial desire was to write an article about the murder of Gable's sister, Diane, and how it affected his life and wrestling. I was nervous, but I had a job to do, and I did it. That went well, so I eventually asked him about this book idea . . . and he said yes! Thus, I was given the opportunity to write a book with and about my childhood sports hero.

This has been one of the most exciting experiences of my life. Dan Gable has now gone from favorite sports figure to friend. And I can say this: as great as Dan Gable has always been as my favorite sports figure, he's an even better friend.

Growing Up

My father always had a proud look in his eye when people would ask him, "When did you know your son was going to be a great wrestler?" The story he always told in response goes like this:

I was born on October 25, 1948, in Waterloo, Iowa, and our family's house at that time was small. Soon after being brought home from the hospital, my father, Mack, heard me crying in my crib one night. When he made his way from the bedroom to my crib, he found me on my back, fighting to get off of it. I was actually bridging up on my head to get off my back.

Even at just a couple of days old, I wanted nothing to do with being on my back.

■ ■ ■

As I became a toddler, my parents' drinking sometimes led to yelling and even violence. They were not alcoholics, but we had occasional visits from the local police. For whatever reason, I took to sucking my thumb and twisting my hair around my finger.

When my parents went out for the evening, I would sit by the front window, waiting for them to return, with my thumb in my mouth and my finger in my hair. I think I worried because when they were at home, I at least knew they were there, which was a little bit of a comfort. When they would go out though, I worried about them and when they would come home. So, like lots of kids, I sucked my thumb, but I twisted my hair too.

Though unlike most, this habit continued into first grade and even took on a new and somewhat odd twist. I would sit at my desk and suck my thumb with my left hand and play with the hair of the person in front of me with my right hand. My teacher tried to get me to stop and ended up having to chase me around the classroom.

My parents also tried different ideas to get me to stop and even got my pediatrician involved. He gave my parents this stuff to put on my thumb that tasted awful. I just sucked the bad-tasting stuff off and kept on sucking my thumb.

Then it stopped. There was no great or profound solution other than me deciding to stop sucking my thumb. I guess I just snapped out of it or no longer needed that habit. Either way, my parents and teacher were relieved.

■ ■ ■

The cornstalks swayed in the gentle Iowa summer breeze above me. I was about four years old and was hiding in a cornfield, giggling as my mother, Katie, and my big sister, Diane, called my name. They were searching the stalks for me, but whenever they got too close, I scurried deeper into the field. The corn was about six feet high, so it was hard to find me, and I knew it. I was determined not to be found. They were pretty mad at me, and rightfully so.

Earlier that day, I sat in the backseat of our family's convertible as my mom and sister drove down a long road flanked by cornfields. It was a perfect day for a drive with the top of the car down. I was bored just sitting there, so I grabbed Diane's purse and started playing with it. I held it up in the air. The wind from the drive caught it, and it went flying away.

My mother immediately hit the brakes and Diane started to chastise me. I knew I was in trouble, so I did the only thing I could think of and ran off to hide in the cornfield. My mom and Diane quickly found the purse in the ditch next to the road, but finding me was another question. The late-season cornstalks were a perfect place for a little boy to hide, and so the search began.

It took them over an hour to finally find me, and when they did, I was really in trouble. This being many decades ago, the punishment was fast and swift. Let's just say there were definitely consequences.

■ ■ ■

My cornfield adventure was not my first, nor my last. I was never one to hurt people or do anything illegal, but I was a little devil. I certainly kept my parents on their toes.

On one occasion, when I was about five years old, our family made a trip to Black's department store in downtown Waterloo. Back then, the elevators were run by an operator. As the four of us crowded into the store's elevator with several strangers, the operator asked, "Which floor, please?"

I was the smallest in the group and knew where we were going, and I quickly yelled out, "Fifth floor . . . bastard!" Swearing was a common part of my parents' vocabulary, but my mother quickly shushed me, and my father scowled, embarrassed. No one else said anything as the elevator moved slowly from floor to floor. At each level, a bell sounded and upon reaching the fifth floor, the elevator stopped, and the door opened. Some people walked out, and I followed them. Then I looked back and saw that my family was still on the elevator as the doors were closing. They were angry with me for embarrassing them, and stayed on the elevator to teach me a lesson. Things were certainly different then than they are today.

I was so mad and upset. When I turned back around, there was an older lady bent over right in front of me. I just reacted and took a chomp on her rear. To this day I don't really remember why. She screamed, and that was the end for me. I knew I was in really big trouble.

A small crowd of store employees and shoppers came quickly to see what all the fuss was about. I had just bitten a complete stranger and was now in the hands of even more strangers. Fear began to wash over me, and I didn't know what to do. I was scared to death.

Finally, my parents and sister came back to the fifth floor to claim me, and when they found out that I had bitten a lady, they were even madder than they were before. This being the 1950s, when we got out to the car, my father popped me on the head with his ring finger. Later at home, my mom used a ruler to show her displeasure.

■ ■ ■

As I mentioned earlier, my parents occasionally became a little hostile toward one another after a few beers. Most of the time this was limited to shouting matches, but the police did make quite a few trips to our residence to settle things down and step in when needed.

One winter night though, my parents were having a little scuffle after a few drinks, and it escalated to the point where the police came to our home. Normally, the police left after calming things down. This night, however, the police took my father with them and put him in the squad car. Being in early elementary school and not understanding the situation, I was quite upset. But I had a plan. One of the police officers who took my father away was a neighbor of ours, and he had a son in my class at school. I was going to teach this particular police officer a lesson.

The police officer's son and I always walked home together after school. The next day, as we were walking home, I wrestled him to the ground, tied his wrists together, and escorted him to his front door. That night, the police officer made another stop at our house. This time, though, I was the topic of conversation.

I certainly got in trouble for that one. I later found out that my father's visit to the police station that night was just to get him out of the house for a few hours to settle down. There were no charges against him, and he wasn't actually arrested. They just played a friendly card game to get him back in the right frame of mind.

I learned a valuable lesson that day: make sure you have all your facts before reacting.

■ ■ ■

Like many young boys, I considered getting a haircut to be on the same scale as getting a tooth pulled, with the haircut maybe even leading the way in things I hated. My mother gave me my first haircuts to save money. Eventually though, there came a time when she wanted to take me to the barbershop for my haircut.

The day of my first barbershop haircut, I rode in the backseat of the convertible as my mother and older sister drove me to a Waterloo barbershop. It was cold out, so we had to keep the roof up as we drove. I did not want to get my hair cut, and I was going to make it as impossible as I could. I had been planning the whole car ride, so when my mother parked in front of the barbershop, I was ready.

When my mom and Diane got out of the car, I quickly pushed down the two lock buttons on the inside of the door. My mother had left the keys inside the car, and since it was cold outside, the windows were up. It was just *click, click,* and I was locked inside. No haircut!

I was feeling pretty good about myself, locked in the car for the moment. Outside, my mother, Diane, and the barber, along with several of his other customers, created quite a scene as they tried, without success, to get me to unlock the doors. This went on for some time until I realized I was getting cold. But before I gave in, I heard a click, and the door popped open.

My father had the spare key, and was I in trouble! Spankings were allowed, and I got one that day. I definitely deserved it.

After that though, I was immediately put back in the car and taken home. Victory! I may have gotten a spanking, but I didn't end up getting a haircut.

■ ■ ■

To teach a young hellion like me some lessons, my parents turned to the Young Men's Christian Association as a place to instill good values and help burn off some of my childhood energy. This was where I was first introduced to several different sports, including wrestling. My first days at the YMCA led to another incident of childhood antics, however.

I had just gotten done with wrestling practice, and it had gone really well for me. I was in a good mood and was waiting for my father to pick me up in front of the YMCA. Unfortunately I ran into a problem: the kid that I had just wrestled was hassling me. The match had been pretty one-sided, and now he wanted to fight me. I tried to do the right thing and said no to fighting, which was a positive step for me. This kid punched me then, and that was more than I could take, so we began to brawl.

My young nemesis took control at first, but I regained it and quickly began to dominate the fight, just as I had the wrestling match. Even at that age, I had good instincts, and I got a good hold of this kid. Our fight continued until our two fathers stepped in to end things.

We later became friends, and we both wondered how long our dads had watched before they stepped in. After all, back in those days, no one jumped in to break up fights right away.

Tunnel Vision

Fifty-plus years is a long time to have an emotion locked away. When unlocked, a buried experience can come back as if it had happened yesterday. One of my earliest experiences as an athlete and one of my first coaching lessons took place at the University of Iowa's old swimming pool, located in the former field house.

In 2011, the University of Iowa was refurbishing its sports complex, Carver-Hawkeye Arena. Due to its construction, the Hawkeye wrestling team was forced to temporarily move into the historic North Gym in the old field house. It was nice though, and the university did an excellent job making sure there were weights, bleachers, and plenty of mat space. It was a good set up.

The head coach, Tom Brands, and wrestling team members proudly showed me their new home-away-from-home and then brought me downstairs to the locker room. I had been in this place before, many years ago. The echo was the same, and the long tunnel from the locker room to the swimming pool was eerily identical to what it had been like five decades prior: dark, long, and somewhat lonely.

What was odd is that my office had been in this building for many years. When I returned from the 1972 Olympics, I served as the assistant wrestling coach at the University of Iowa for a few years before becoming head coach, and for several of those years, we trained in this very building. Yet during that time, I had never gone downstairs to the pool's locker room.

In that moment, standing there in 2011, a memory surfaced just as fresh as it had ever been. Like many athletes, my story began at a local YMCA. My parents saw the Waterloo YMCA as a good place for their lively son to work off some energy while being surrounded by friends and positive role models. It didn't take me long to latch on to a variety of different activities offered at the YMCA, but it wasn't wrestling I gravitated to at first as a youngster. Instead, I started swimming.

Swimming was fun, but competitive swimming was serious business. There were a lot of sports offered at the YMCA—boxing, wrestling, basketball—and I played them all, but we had a great swim team. We competed on a weekly basis against swimmers from other YMCA teams throughout Iowa.

This was where I had my first taste of winning . . . and I liked it, a lot. I played baseball in the spring and summer and had been on a team that won a city championship, but swimming was really my own thing. I regularly won my events, and as the state championship meet approached, I alone stood undefeated in the backstroke and did well in the individual medley. The divisional meet, and then the state finals, gave me my initial experience of being a champion. When I finished first in the state in the backstroke, I knew I really liked winning. I had made a name for myself with my prowess in the pool. As an eleven-year-old, this was something I enjoyed.

Throughout the season, one of my teammates, Tom Penaluna, was always in my rearview mirror in the backstroke, both at practice and in competition. He was always right there, just behind me. At the state finals, it was the same in the backstroke, which wasn't even his best event.

After the state championship, we had a six-week break from competition, though we all continued to train. After those six weeks, we returned to the University of Iowa pool to compete in the regional championships. The meet included the best swimmers from Iowa and several surrounding states, but I was ready to keep my winning streak alive.

Something else happened, though: I took second place in the backstroke to Tom.

This was my first real taste of losing in my whole life. I had finished fourth in the state in the individual medley, but I had never experienced losing in the backstroke. The initial sting of defeat was made even worse by the fact that I had lost to Tom. He was a great kid who is very successful in business today. But I beat him every day in practice and at every competition. Yet, he had somehow beaten me. I took it very hard.

I had gotten used to watching my family and friends always jumping for joy in the stands after each victory in my string of wins. When I lost to Tom, I looked out from the pool and found my loved ones. They were still beaming with pride and clapping, but the emotion was different from when I won. Gone was the jumping for joy. It was replaced with smiles and offers of compassion and support.

I felt that I had let everyone down. The dagger of that pain was almost too much for me to bear as an eleven-year-old. Fifty years later, when I stood again in the locker room with Tom Brands and the 2011 wrestling team and looked down the tunnel to the pool, I felt that sting all over again. The feeling of losing and disappointing everyone washed over me again as though it was yesterday.

The drive home to Waterloo that night after the swim meet was a long one. As my family made the ninety-minute ride, I sat in the backseat of the car, staring out at the blackness. I remained inconsolable. I replayed the race over and over in my mind. I had to figure out what went wrong, how I had been beaten by someone I had never lost to in nearly twenty races.

When we got home, my mom sat me down and set me straight.

She didn't pull any punches, and she let me know that I had made everyone proud, even in defeat. In my mind I had let everyone down. Yet they all still loved me, and my mom let me know that everything was going to be okay and that I had not disappointed them. I quickly straightened up.

Looking back now, I can see how this experience offered me my first glimpse into a world that not all athletes live in. Those who achieve the highest level of greatness in their lives often do so because they have people who love and support them. People who only try to accomplish something for themselves can miss out on how rewarding it is to have people around them who love them and care about them and support their goals. On that night many years ago, I didn't have any answers for why I lost. But I did know that my family loved and supported me.

Someone later explained to me that, at that age, everyone's bodies are developing at a different rate. I lost that race because Tom had physically matured more than I had over those six weeks between competitions. I probably would not have figured that out on my own at that age, but it was important to understand. It helped me deal with that loss.

This lesson about maturity and developing bodies also became a valuable tool for me over the years as an athlete and later as a coach at Iowa. A college coach may be recruiting an athlete who is in a certain weight class, and they are looking at him at the size he is in high school. It's important to remember that this person is probably not fully physically developed yet. The coach needs to do a lot of research to get the best idea as to where this athlete will eventually compete a few years down the line. They need to meet the family, talk to the parents and siblings. That will give them a good idea as to when an athlete they're recruiting may stop growing.

Those recruiting someone for a position in the business world should take a similar approach. They need to do as much research as possible to see if this person is a good fit for the company and, if so, how they will best fit. What they see at one moment may very well not be who they will be working with in a year, five years, or ten years.

Even though I've been using lessons I learned that night at the University of Iowa pool my entire career, I hadn't thought about the event itself in years. My visit to the pool locker room and the tunnel in 2011 brought it all back like it was yesterday, even after fifty years. I'm glad it did. It was a good reminder of lessons learned in life.

3

Molly Putz

One winter night in 1962, a single set of headlights broke through the immense darkness of a slowing snowstorm just outside Waterloo, Iowa. The car moved through the twelve inches of snow with relative ease as our family drove home from one of my earliest wrestling matches, a junior high showdown with a neighboring school that had not gone the way I planned.

I was pinning my opponent when the kid bridged up on his neck and somehow rolled me over to my back and pinned me. I wasn't sure what exactly happened. Years later as a coach, one of my athletes used the same move, so I had the opportunity to understand the mechanics, but at the time, I was so upset! The whole way home, I sat in the back of the car and fumed over the loss. I just couldn't figure out what went wrong.

When we got home, I dragged myself into the house. I was still angry and confused over losing and pouted as I moved from room to room, until I wound up in my bedroom. I could see from my window how the snow had piled up outside. With a deep sigh, I did the only thing I could think of: lie down and sulk. After all, sulking and feeling sorry for oneself often appears to be the only viable option when dealing with sadness, frustration, or any other negative emotion for many young people in junior high.

Still, I was pouting and feeling sorry for myself in the home of Mack and Katie Gable, where such behavior was not tolerated.

Eventually my mother entered my bedroom, and rather than coddling her disappointed son, she took a more aggressive approach.

"You know what you are?" she asked, hands on her hips. "You're a Molly Putz!"

"Molly Putz" was a term my mom used for us when we were feeling sorry for ourselves.

My mom continued, "You need to stop feeling sorry for yourself and be a man. You know what? The driveway needs to be shoveled, and I'd like you—no, wait, I am telling you—to go outside and get the shoveling done."

I was mad. My mother had just called me out, it was cold outside, I was tired, and I was still mad that I lost. But I put my boots and jacket on and went outside and grabbed the shovel. The cold air bit my face as I scooped the first pile of snow and tossed it to the side. Then I did it again, and then a third time. As I scooped, something started to churn in my stomach, like a monster looking for a way out. This monster was anger and determination, and I was about to unleash it all over our neighborhood.

I attacked our driveway. I shoveled snow so fast it looked like I was a snow blower. They weren't invented yet, or at least we didn't have one, so it was just the shovel and me. I was almost running as I completely focused on removing the snow from our driveway. Then, when I was done, I went to our neighbors and shoveled their driveway. Then I went on to the next house.

My anger had turned into something positive. I didn't want to be a Molly Putz, so I kept shoveling the driveways on my street in Waterloo until I worked myself into exhaustion. It felt good to work out that anger, so I just kept shoveling and shoveling until it was gone. That night I proved I was not a Molly Putz.

Throughout my childhood and youth, my desire to never be called that name often drove me. To help their children avoid becoming Molly Putzes, my parents created a home environment based on hard work. Since my father owned his own business, my sister, Diane, and I learned the importance of hard work early in life. There were no Molly Putzes in the Gable family.

■ ■ ■

In the summer of 1965, I had just won the Iowa state high school championships in the 103-pound weight class. With summer casting hazy, hot, and humid days over Waterloo, I continued to lift weights to get stronger, but my father had an even better idea. He was always looking out for me, and supported my wrestling career. I was stronger than I looked, and my father knew how much I loved lifting weights, but he told me he had a tougher training program for me that summer.

My father set me up with a job working for Martinson Construction, a company that is still in business today. They create masonry walls for new homes being built. My day consisted of manual labor, and it was hard work, especially in the summer months when the heat would reach close to one hundred degrees, while mixing with humidity.

In setting this up, my father went behind my back and asked the owner, Jerry Martinson, if I could work for the company as a way to train for the coming year's wrestling season. The kicker was that my father would give Martinson whatever I earned during the week. Jerry would then pay me and not have to take it out of his own pocket.

I remain thankful to this day for my father's willingness to pay for this summer job. It shows the insight he had into who I was at that time. We all need to have people in our lives looking after us, and we need to do the same for other people. My father was looking out for me in setting this up. He didn't tell me the truth about how he arranged it, allowing me to believe I had just been hired. When I eventually learned the truth years later, I was amazed.

My first day on the job, I kept thinking about what my parents had taught me about work. They always said that, when you get a job, you have to work very hard and very smart. If you didn't do those two things, you'd get fired. That made me real nervous. Up until this point in my life, I had earned money by working for my father's real estate construction company. I'd paint, fix things, and just be an overall gofer. It was helpful, but my father knew that working for Martinson would help me learn more about hard work.

On my first day, another new employee and I were put into a basement where the cement walls were already in place. There were two piles of sand, and we were given shovels and instructed to move the piles and make them even with the top of the first row of cement blocks. The basement was hot, musty, filled with dust, and offered no form of ventilation. Those things were not important to me, though. I wanted to work hard and not be a Molly Putz. I started working and just attacked the sand, working like I did that night with the snow shoveling. I just went a hundred miles an hour. I wanted to get it done right and done quickly.

In thirty minutes, I completed a task that normally took two hours. When I was done, I was breathing heavy and drenched in sweat. My hands were battered with blisters from the shovel, but I felt great: I was working hard. When I looked over to the other pile, though, the other new employee I'd come down into the basement with was nowhere to be found. Perhaps intimidated by his younger and smaller shoveling partner, or maybe just by the nature of the hard work, the other man had quit on the spot. Either way, I was alone, and my boss told me to move the other pile of sand. Not a problem for me, and I worked with a vengeance. When I was done with that, I went to my boss and asked, "What's next?"

Next, they had me unload a truckload of cement blocks. They were heavy and I had to carry them over to a pile. It was tough, but I just kept working as hard as I could. I eventually went on to do all kinds of hard manual labor. I was always moving blocks, digging ditches, mixing cement, moving wooden planks, and swinging a sledgehammer. It was great. I became a workaholic.

After about a week on the job, my father received a visit from Jerry Martinson. He told my father, "Mr. Gable, I can't continue to have you pay for your son to work with us. I appreciate what you're doing for him, but we just can't continue to do this with you paying us to pay him. We'll pay him."

Regardless of who was paying me, I quickly became a commodity to the company. The hard work continued as the method to my madness became obvious to the older employees. They knew I was using this job as a way to work out. They understood my goals and purpose, moving fast while doing difficult tasks, so they made sure to keep me busy with hard work. If things got slow, they would have me move a pile of cement blocks from the front of a house to the back, then back to the front again. Some of them were corner blocks, so they were even heavier and bigger than the regular blocks. They always found something hard for me to do.

The job was perfect for me. In fact, I saw it more as a chance to work out than earn money, but getting to do both at the same time was the perfect match. Adding to the physical labor of the job, I started challenging the men on the crew to wrestling matches when lunch was over. Sometimes the men would take me up on my offer, but the matches always ended the same way. They were all quite a bit bigger than me, but none of them could ever beat me.

My days were exhausting. I worked this way from seven in the morning until about five in the evening. In addition, three days a week, our wrestling team had open mat wrestling practice at the high school. So I'd go from working all day and then wrestle for a good solid hour. By 6:30 P.M., I was home, where I ate dinner and immediately fell asleep. My alarm would sound the next morning, and then I was back at it again. I even worked on Saturdays for five hours and would often run to and from the job site. To top it off, my hands were all torn up from carrying things and always had blisters.

I was a hard worker before taking the job with Martinson, but over the summer, my level of intensity increased. It ultimately paid off, as I put on about seven pounds of muscle. Combined with continuing to wrestle, I was ready to crank it up on the mats that coming winter. I have never gotten so strong in a short period of time as I did that summer. I got more physical, continued to practice wrestling, earned people's respect, and earned some money. I loved the summer of 1965.

Friendship Forever

It was 1975, the height of the Cold War, and the gym in Bloomsburg, Pennsylvania, was overfilled, literally, with spectators waving American flags, as chants of "U-S-A" rained down from the enthusiastic pro-American audience. The Soviet national wrestling team was in town and having its way with the Americans, but that did not ruin the high-spirited atmosphere of the event.

The gym had been overbooked, and the mat was in the very middle of the space. When the wrestlers left the mat, they were practically falling on top of people. It was extremely loud and nearly impossible to hear any one person.

In the middle of this clamor, Doug Moses stepped to the mat to battle his opponent from the Soviet Union. The match came down to the wire, and through the screams and cheering, Doug could somehow hear one voice carved out through the noisy gym. It was his childhood best friend and the man who coached the American team that night: me.

"I only heard Dan," Doug recalls of that night. "That was all I heard throughout the whole match. Dan coached me to the win. It was a little strange because it remains one of the loudest experiences of my life. I couldn't hear anything and the noise was so loud it pierced my ears, but through it all, I could hear Dan."

The fact that he could hear me in the frenzied gym was not a surprise to Doug, then or now. He is really more of a brother than a friend, and we've known each other a long time. In all that time, it has always been about wrestling with us. Doug is a year younger than me, and we became friends through junior high wrestling in Waterloo, where everything was about wrestling. We were no different from anyone else in that respect, except that the two of us took our dedication to the sport to an extreme.

When I entered high school as a tenth grader in the fall of 1963, Wrestling Coach Bob Siddens felt that he could trust me to open the gym doors in the morning before school began, so he gave me the keys to the school. I really wanted to work out, and my family lived across the street from Waterloo West High School, so each morning I was there opening the school's gym at 6:00 A.M. Alone, I would enter the darkened gym, my steps echoing as I walked to the lights. I'd run, lift weights, drill, and shower, and I was always ready for school to begin. It would have been lonely for a less motivated young man, but wrestling is a somewhat lonely person's sport anyway. Plus, I was always focused, even at 6:00 A.M.

A year later, when Doug moved up to the high school, I had an early morning workout partner, even if it meant waking up thirty minutes earlier each day. I'd get up and drive out to Doug's house and pick him up. Then we'd get back to the school and get our early morning workouts in.

"It was every day," Doug remembers. "Those winter mornings in Waterloo were often below zero, but Dan would be there to pick me up and we'd get those workouts in. A lot of running, lifting weights, and wrestling, every day."

During the summer months, the two of us put in miles of running under the blazing hot sun. We would go up the small gravel roads of rural Iowa, with one of us running while the other drove the car. Then we would switch places and drive back. Once, when we were out at a wrestling camp in Mason City, Iowa, after a full day's wrestling session, we took the car and found an old road to run along.

When it was Doug's turn to run, I rolled up the car's windows to increase the heat so I could stay loose and warm for my turn. After a few miles, I stopped the car and Doug took over driving back to town while I ran.

Doug was wearing one of those plastic suits that were popular at the time, to cause him to sweat as much as possible. The problem was, he was sweating too much. As he drove the car, his legs and hands started to cramp up. His foot continued to press down on the gas pedal, and the car sped up, its tires spitting gravel and dirt.

"Doug! Doug!" I yelled. "Slow down!"

Doug was delirious and couldn't get his foot off the gas pedal. He was close to unconsciousness, and his body was cramping all over. I was able to get the car stopped and could tell immediately that Doug was in shock. I dragged him out of the car and started to pull his clothes off, while pouring small amounts of water in his mouth. When Doug started to improve, I put him in the back of the car and, with the windows rolled down, drove as fast as I could back to the gym. Once there, I dragged Doug into the showers and turned them on.

"This was a long time before the rules of weight management hit wrestling," Doug says of the incident. "We never thought of going to a hospital either. We knew I was extremely dehydrated. I had dropped about ten pounds of water weight. Dan knew I needed water, and I remember just lying on the floor of the showers and drinking the water pouring onto me. I stayed there on the floor until my body got better."

While that was probably the most harrowing run of all, the miles we charted over the years of our lifelong friendship could never be measured. Neither could the hours the two of us spent wrestling. Most of those hours were in my family's basement, where I had a twelve by twelve foot mat. The room was really small, and we were crashing into walls all the time, but we were wrestling and learning how to finish moves quickly, and that's what mattered. If we weren't wrestling in my basement, it was in the yard or even on a strip of grass. Anywhere we could wrestle, we did.

Doug's girlfriend lived across the street from my family, and when Doug would go over to visit her, I called their house to get him to come over for an hour or two of wrestling. Sometimes Doug tried parking in a hiding place, so I wouldn't know he was there. But whenever that happened, I was still able to find his car, and then him. It never took much for me to get Doug to break away for some wrestling. His girlfriend's brother was older than us, and he was on the wrestling team at Waterloo West. She never got upset about Doug leaving her to wrestle with me. She understood our dedication. Once we were done, he'd shower and go back to his girlfriend's house, and I would either find another way to work out or go fishing.

Even when my family brought Doug along on our family fishing trip to Canada, the two of us spent more time wrestling on the grass outside the cabin than actually fishing. "The Gables always treated me like I was a member of the family," Doug says. "Dan and I were always together and most of that time were wrestling. He watched out for me so I didn't get into any trouble. Dan was not one to go to parties, and if he did, he'd show up covered in sweat, and if it was winter, he'd be covered in snow because he'd run to the party."

On one occasion, though, I was the one who needed the rescuing. Back in the 1960s, the rivalry between Waterloo West High and Cedar Falls High was more than intense. Groups from the two schools spent most weekends in some kind of altercation, usually starting at a pizza parlor or a soda shop. One warm summer night, the athletes from Waterloo West were at a local pizza place enjoying the evening. When we left, I went outside ahead of my friends. Suddenly, guys from Cedar Falls surrounded me. They started pushing me around and hitting me, and the next thing I knew, I was on the ground being kicked in the head. It was rough, and I don't know how many more times I could have handled that.

Within seconds, the pizza place emptied, and a fight ensued as the Waterloo West guys fought to get inside the circle to rescue me. Doug was so enraged by the attack that he ran over to a street sign and ripped it right out of the ground. He began swinging the street sign over his head and screaming. It was amazing. Seeing that, our rivals quickly scattered, and one of the Waterloo West athletes scooped me up and got me away from the scene of the fight.

Doug says of the incident now, "You don't know what you are capable of until you are put in a dangerous situation. Dan was my best friend, and I think my adrenaline to help him gave me the strength to pull that sign out of the ground. There is no other way to describe it."

Sometimes in life, it's ripping a street sign out of the ground to help a friend, while other times, it is simply being in their presence during a tough time. When Doug was a senior in high school, I drove up from Ames to support him and the Waterloo West wrestling team at the annual state tournament. When you are in high school, being a state champion is the goal. It's what you work for all year, and there can only be one state champion in each weight class.

Doug was undefeated his senior year, and in the state semifinals faced the one person who actually had beaten him the year before. He defeated this tough competitor with ease and then coasted into the state final. However, by focusing on his semifinals match and overlooking his finals opponent, Doug was not ready to give a top performance. Doug had beaten this particular opponent a couple times before, and so was probably not taking the match as seriously as he should. I kept telling him to stay focused and not to take his opponent too lightly. Unfortunately, the semifinal match was his highlight, and when the time ran out on the state final match, Doug was beaten. He finished in second place and felt crushed. No one wrestles to be second, certainly not Doug Moses.

"When the match was over, and I was real upset, Dan was there," Doug remembers. "I don't think Dan said a thing. He knew what I was feeling. He knew I was upset and down. But the thing about our relationship is that Dan didn't need to say anything. I didn't need him to say anything. I just needed to know he was there. Isn't that what best friends are about?"

Life Change

On an unusually warm day in the early spring of 2011, my home phone rang. A prison official told me that John Thomas Kyle, the man who had murdered my older sister, Diane, in 1964, was close to death. The news hit me like a punch in the stomach. My throat tightened, my chest felt heavy, and I just broke down.

I became even more emotional when the official told me that Kyle expressed remorse over what had occurred in our home that May night long ago. He said that he wished he had not killed Diane and that she was a nice girl. That ultimately helped me deal with my emotions, but it also brought back the memories of that weekend.

I had always felt something was just a little off about my neighbor, John Thomas Kyle. We weren't friends, and we traveled in different crowds as students at Waterloo West High School, though we were in the same grade. I was a noted jock, and Kyle was close to becoming a dropout. One day, however, in the early spring of 1964, about a month after I had won my first high school state wrestling championship at the age of fifteen, we met up as we walked to school. Kyle brought up my sister, and his talk quickly turned inappropriate. He said things of a sexual nature about her, which was weird and uncomfortable. At the time though, I didn't think much of it.

Diane was nineteen and had a boyfriend. She had tried the college route after graduating from high school, but she didn't really like it and returned home to be the secretary for my father's success-ful real estate company. She was very social and had lots of friends who were involved with the wrestling program at the high school, and she followed my wrestling career closely.

Memorial Day weekend came about a month later, and our family decided to take a fishing trip to Harper's Ferry, Iowa, an area off the Mississippi River. Diane begged our parents to let her spend a por-tion of the weekend at home alone, and they reluctantly gave in. The three of us left Diane behind and focused on the main part of the trip: fishing.

Diane was supposed to meet up with us on Saturday, but she was late, which was not like her. My father called home, but there was no answer. We began to grow concerned. My father then started calling neighbors, one of whom reported that Diane's car was still in the driveway. This neighbor also noted hearing a television from in-side the locked house. Growing ever more worried, my father asked this neighbor to investigate further and to get inside the house. The three of us just sat there in our car next to the phone booth, waiting for the call, worried. It seemed to take forever.

Finally, the phone rang. My father spoke few words and just lis-tened, then started to choke up. My mother was frantic to know what happened. The tension was thick between them, and I could see it growing.

After a long moment, my father dropped the phone and just said, "She's not alive."

In that moment of uncertainty, my mother took off running back to our family's rented cabin, away from us. I did the only thing I could think of: I chased after my mother. When I got back to the cabin, she was crumpled on the floor. Her hands were wrapped around her hair, and she was banging her head on the floor, scream-ing. She was completely out of control. Her face and her head were bleeding badly.

My father came in and quickly took control, calming her down. Then we all got in the car and took off back to Waterloo. We didn't even bring any of our things. An eerie silence overtook us as we drove home that night. The only sounds were the humming of the car engine and my mother's crying. Suddenly, I remembered my conversation with Kyle from a month before and broke the silence.

I told my parents that I might know something about this. My father immediately pulled over, yanked me out of the car, threw me up against it, and sort of slapped me around. He was so upset that he was almost out of control. I told him about my weird conversation with Kyle and how creepy it was. After that, my dad hugged me, and we got back in the car. We went straight to the first police station we could find.

Within hours, our home had gone from being a picture of Americana to one of gothic terror. The authorities immediately tracked Kyle down, and he quickly confessed to the murder. He was able to describe the grisly and disturbing scene inside our house with chilling precision.

Friday night, Diane had invited some friends over to our house for a party. After everyone had gone home, Diane retired to her room. Kyle then broke in through the back door and found Diane lying innocently on her bed. He woke her with his sexual intentions, but Diane adamantly refused the young man's advances. Enraged, Kyle raped, stabbed, and beat Diane to death.

Diane's murder became a turning point in my life. This horrific moment jump-started a fierce fire inside me, which carried me through the days and years that followed. I had to say goodbye to my sister, whom I admired, and was forced to find within myself the will to save my family from being torn apart.

I refused to allow Kyle to destroy my entire family or create a cancer of hatred within my own soul. I never hated Kyle or his family. He was sentenced to life without parole, and I felt he deserved that.

I saw members of his family around town, and I never blamed them. This event happened, and it was terrible, but I could not let it consume my life. But my parents were falling apart, and I had to do something to help them.

My first step toward saving my family was taking the lead in some of the most difficult parts of moving forward. When we returned to Waterloo and discovered just how much blood there was at the scene of the crime and the condition of Diane's body, my parents refused to go inside the house. We stayed with my grandmother in her small apartment for several days until I stepped up. We had lost Diane, and I couldn't bear the thought of losing our home as well. So I went to my parents and told them that I wanted to go home. They didn't want to, but I kept pushing it until we finally did.

We had the carpet torn up and we threw away all of the knives and other silverware because we didn't know what had actually been the murder weapon. No one went into Diane's room. And my parents' drinking just got worse. They would drink and fight and blame. It was insane.

Around this time, my father acquired a habit that to others would seem disturbing, but for him it brought some peace. He started going over to the fire station several nights a week, which was located across the street from the local jail. From the fire station's roof, my father could see Kyle walking around inside the jail. One of my dad's best friends at the firehouse gave him an unloaded rifle. My father would take the scoped rifle up to the fire station's roof and aim it at Kyle from across the street. There were never any bullets in that rifle, but my father would put Kyle in the crosshairs of his scope and pull the trigger.

One night, as I lay in my bedroom trying to sleep, a screaming match between my parents led to my mother blurting out, "If I had raised Diane to be a whore, she'd be alive!" Hearing that, I leapt from my bed and charged into the kitchen, where my parents stood, filled with their cocktail of anger, rage, guilt, and despair. I knew our family was at a crossroads. My parents were going to fail unless I figured out a way to save them. We had to move forward, and this had to stop. That night, my instincts took over, and I told my parents I was moving into Diane's room. They didn't try to stop me.

I moved into Diane's room that very night. It never disturbed me to be in there. I thought about Diane, but I didn't dwell on what had happened. This was now my room. After that, we turned my old bedroom into an office for my parents. My mother started helping with my dad's business. The healing was underway.

However, I understood that the next step in our collective recovery needed to follow swiftly. Our family needed a new direction, a new focus, to keep from dwelling on Diane's death. So I turned my parents' attention to something that they all loved: wrestling and, above all, me. I had to become the best wrestler possible to give my parents something else to focus on. My approach to saving our family worked, and I ended up dominating Iowa prep wrestling through the mid-1960s, before moving on to Iowa State.

All these years later, I still remember my sister. I remember her smile, her kindness, and playing with her when we were young. I mostly remember the greatest gift my sister gave me: her life and joy when she was alive. I think of Diane every day, and I remain appreciative of the inner drive I developed after her death. That inner drive helped keep our family together, helped me win a gold medal at the Olympics, and paved the way for the rest of my life and career.

You move on, but you never really get over an experience like Diane's death. Kyle says he wishes he had not killed Diane because she was such a nice girl. That helps, but the memories are still there. It's just the way life is.

A Friend in Need

One night in February 1966, as the gusty Iowa wind whipped through the streets of Waterloo, the crowd in McElroy Auditorium leapt to its feet. A young man from Waterloo West High School, undefeated in his high school career, had just won the state wrestling championship at 120 pounds and brought the fans to a frenzy. They had watched this young man for three years as a member of the school's champion wrestling team, and he was now standing at the top of his own weight class and, for the third year in a row, had not dropped a single bout. The young man's name was Marty Dickey.

Marty's journey to his senior year state championship was full of dips, turns, detours, and one major obstacle: me. As sophomores, we both wrestled in the 95-pound weight class, but I secured the varsity spot, pushing Marty to JV. Marty finished the year undefeated, but he couldn't attend the state tournament because each school was only allowed to enter one wrestler per weight class. Our junior year was the same story for Marty: undefeated, but stuck behind me at 103 pounds.

Undaunted, Marty continued to work hard, and when the 1966 season began, he and I weighed the same again, this time 120 pounds. As the two-time defending state champion, I beat Marty for the varsity spot again, but things were about to change. Our coach approached me and asked me to drop to the 112-pound weight class and open the 120 spot for Marty.

The idea was perfect as far as I was concerned. Marty was my friend, and I wanted to do what I could to help him. All of my life my best friends have been people that had something I lacked. Marty was no different. He gave me something I never had on my own: a social life. I wanted to do something to return the favor.

I always had a hard time getting away from the one-dimensional world of constant wrestling. Marty was much more outgoing than me. I was shy by nature, and he was able to get me outside of myself. He introduced me to girls, and he included me in his fun. He was good for me because, without him, I would never have had any fun off the mat.

Marty and I met through wrestling when we were attending different junior high schools. One evening, I invited him over to my house. As my parents welcomed Marty into our home, I sat there, fidgeting. After a few minutes of talking, I asked Marty if he wanted to go downstairs and lift weights. Marty declined what he probably thought was a very strange offer from someone he barely knew.

"But that was Dan," Marty says of the incident now. "He always wanted to train, always thinking about how to get better, and he had and still has an incredible ability to see and plan for the future."

I was never really able to sit back and relax in those days. Just after the state wrestling tournament our sophomore year, I had a group of friends, which included Marty, over at my house to watch the Waterloo West basketball team on television as they played their first round of the state tournament. As the other guys watched the game, there was the constant sound of grunting from the back of the living room. I was working out in preparation for next year's state wrestling tournament.

"Dan was driving us crazy," Marty remembers. "He was making all of this noise, and we were trying to watch the game. Finally I said, 'Hey Gable, shut up! We're trying to watch the game!'"

I quietly and simply responded, "I have to be ready for Dailey."

Dailey was a wrestler I had a strong chance of facing in the state tournament a year later. I was preparing for that match just days after winning the state title as a tenth grader. My friends responded to that as friends would: they teased me, then kicked me out of my own living room so they could watch the game in peace, while I went on training elsewhere in the house.

Marty always seemed to enjoy giving me a hard time because I was so serious. One of his favorite pastimes was to purposely give incorrect answers whenever I quizzed him for an upcoming vocabulary test. Sometimes the whole gang would be shooting pool, and I would give the words, only to have everyone give the wrong definition, which drove me crazy. I would always start yelling at them for not being prepared, but everyone just laughed. They thought it was funny to see me getting so upset.

It was Marty who dragged the social part of me into the world. Marty loved to meet new people, and he was always doing things to get me to come out of my shell. When we were about sixteen, we liked to drive to local pubs, even though we were underage. We would go in, have a drink, and meet and talk to all of these women that were too old for us. Sometimes we got kicked out, but we always ended up having great conversations with the women outside the bars. It was all just innocent high school fun.

One of Marty's favorite stories about our time in high school was about my black shoes, which I wore all the time, and which everyone thought were ugly. One cold night after wrestling practice, Marty and a few other teammates sat in the school's foyer waiting to head home, when I came walking toward them from the darkened hallway. They had not heard me coming because I was fully dressed, but on my feet were just a pair of white tube socks.

"We asked him what happened to his shoes, and he said someone had stolen them," Marty remembers. "It was hard to believe because Dan had these ugly black shoes, and we used to make fun of him about them."

I always left my shoes outside of my wrestling locker during practice. At the time I thought one of my friends had taken them as a joke, but no one ever came forward and returned them. While to this day I could never understand why anyone would have wanted those ugly shoes, someone else must have really stolen them. I never saw those shoes again.

My friends quickly came up with a solution. They thought it was time for me to join the crowd and get a pair of penny loafers, the popular shoe of the day. One of the guys gave me a piggyback ride to the car so that I didn't have to walk in the snow with just my socks. Then, we all headed to my house. Marty and my friends talked to my father and explained the situation. He gave me twenty bucks, which was a lot of money at the time, for a new pair of shoes, and they took me out and got me a pair of penny loafers. "It was a definite step up from the ugly black shoes," Marty says.

When our group of friends went to parties, people always approached Marty with two questions: Which guy is Gable, and isn't he a little weird? As a true friend would, Marty always managed both questions perfectly.

"People wanted to know who this Dan Gable guy was and I'd point him out," Marty recalls. "So many people would say, 'He doesn't look like much.' I always told those people, 'Put your hands on him, and you'll find out just how much he is.' With a lot of things in life, you hear the saying, 'What you see is what you get.' With Dan, that was not the case. He was small and skinny, so what you saw was not what you were going to get.

"We were all very protective of Dan. You have to really know Dan to 'get him.' He is just so full of energy and intensity that he doesn't sit still very much. He knew what his goals were and maybe that struck people a little odd because he worked so hard and so much. He wasn't weird; he was just always doing something."

This was certainly true of me, especially as a teenager. When we went out with friends to have a couple of drinks, I always wanted to go for a run. It was common for Marty and the other guys to drive the car as I ran beside them. I may have been away from the practice room, but my mind never really left the wrestling mat.

"Dan was always thinking about wrestling," Marty says. "We were at a park one night, and the rest of us were drinking some beers, and Dan decided he needed to go for a run. Well, it's a good thing he did, because while he was running, he saw a couple of police cars that were combing the park. He came back and told us about the police, so we left."

I was so shy in those days that it was Marty who introduced me to girls around town. When I was about sixteen, he introduced me to one particular cute blond young lady. We actually dated a few times, but it didn't last long. According to Marty, the girl was just not very nice to me, so it was okay that it never went anywhere.

"This girl really was sort of a jerk to Dan, and it bothered me," Marty says now. "I saw her and told her, 'Someday Dan Gable is going to be one of the most famous people in the world, and you know what? He's not going to remember you.'"

The ironic thing is, I do still remember her.

One of our group's favorite activities as teenagers was our annual road trip to Missouri to buy fireworks just prior to the Fourth of July. That was where you could buy all of the really good fireworks that were illegal in Iowa. We'd pile in a car and drive as fast as we could, so when we got back home, our parents wouldn't suspect that we'd been on a road trip. There wasn't an interstate back then, and it was just a two-lane road, so we felt that it was a real adventure. After that, on the Fourth of July itself, we would all venture into the woods, where we had an epic firecracker battle. We ran around screaming or just hid behind trees and bushes and threw firecrackers at each other. It was a blast, literally.

Our friendship and loyalty created a solid bond between us during those years. Marty improved as a wrestler by wrestling me in practice, and as I will tell anyone, I became a better and more socially adjusted person because of him. This is why, after Marty's state championship, I fought my way through the crowd to be one of the first people to greet Marty when he came off the mat.

The moment is forever branded in Marty's mind: "There were people everywhere, and I came off the mat, and Dan was there. He had a huge smile on his face, and he shook my hand and said, 'Congratulations, champ!' That is something I will never forget."

I had just won my third state high school championship at 112 pounds and, in doing so, finished my high school career undefeated. But when Marty won his state championship, everyone was so excited that they just rushed down to him. I was more excited about his championship than my own.

Two Clippings

The gym at Hofstra University was rocking. Even the damp, frigid wind whipping through the campus at Hempstead, Long Island, couldn't keep the Flying Dutchmen fans away on this Saturday afternoon in 1969 as the Hofstra wrestlers faced off against Iowa State. Every seat was taken, leaving fans to swarm the floor and sit all the way from the wall to the very edge of the mat, with even more fans packed into the hallways just hoping for a glimpse of the big dual.

I was the defending NCAA national champion at the time, and I remember it was just crazy. We literally had to step over the Hofstra fans as we made our way out to the mat for team introductions.

Like nearly every college in the nation, the fans at Hofstra were creative as the athletes met at center mat for the pre-match handshake. When the announcer introduced an Iowa State wrestler, two claps echoed out in unison. Then, when a home team wrestler's name was announced, the crowd cheered wildly. When my opponent, Hofstra's Marty Willigan, was introduced, something unusual happened, even for one of my matches. I got my two claps, just like everyone else on our team. When Willigan was introduced, the place went absolutely nuts. It was so loud, so intense. I figured they were doing it because they thought he needed some help.

The interesting thing about the noise was that Willigan was deaf. The young man wrestled his whole life and never had the opportunity to hear the fans' cheers. Today, however, Willigan had the chance to give those fans something to really cheer about. Willigan was set on ending my winning streak and shocking the wrestling world.

When it was time to wrestle, I climbed back through the crowd of people and got out to the mat. But to this day, I can't tell you exactly what happened there. I was so focused, and with that crazy environment, I just wrestled. Next thing I knew, the match was over, and I wasn't even certain whose hand had been raised.

There is one thing from that experience that I do remember: exhaustion. When the match ended, I had never been so wiped out in the sport. I climbed off the mat and made my way through the crowd on wobbly legs looking for an empty chair, but there were none to be found. I made my way into the packed hallway. Leaning up against the wall, I slowly slid to the floor and sat, still unaware if I had won.

Eventually, one of my coaches came out and found me. He helped me to my feet, but I was completely drained. I had been exhausted and pained during the match, but I was so focused I didn't even realize it. I just wrestled from whistle to whistle. Then I saw Willigan walking toward us with one of his coaches. He was fresh and talking about the match. Just talking and talking and talking about how next time he would get me. As far as I was concerned, he got me right then. I couldn't believe it. I finally asked my coach if I'd won and he told me I had, 12 to 1. My coach said I did pretty well and had beaten him up pretty good. I wasn't my usual self, but he said I stayed focused. Willigan really gave me a battle.

All these years later, I'm still not exactly sure what made me so exhausted. A number of factors probably played into the way I nearly had to crawl off the mat. Maybe I didn't warm up the right way, or maybe it was just that I'd wrestled someone better than I usually do.

The Cyclones finished off the hosting Flying Dutchmen, and the team headed to Pennsylvania where we would wrestle our next match the following day. When I awoke the next morning, one of my teammates handed me a copy of the New York newspaper that had covered the match. "You need to read this," he said.

I normally didn't like to read newspaper coverage of my wrestling. This time was different, though, because my teammates told me I needed to see the article and what Willigan had said. This is how I first learned just who Marty Willigan was and that he was no regular opponent.

Willigan was a returning senior All-American and had entered our match with an undefeated home match streak. He had never lost at home until he met me. That information was interesting, but it would not have changed anything had I known my opponent's credentials the day before. I had no idea he was that good, but even if I'd known, it wouldn't have made any difference as far as my preparation for the match or the way I approached it. You can't go changing everything you do when you're up against a challenge in life. You stick to what you do and go out and take care of business. I just wrestled like I always did.

It was a quote from Willigan in the article that really caught my attention, though. "He got me this time," Willigan said. "He got me twelve to one. But he's a man, and I'm a man, and next time, it will be different." This was clearly a confident young man who admitted defeat but was certainly not ready to surrender.

That quote sank into my mind. I wanted to remember that bold statement, so after looking around to make sure I was alone, I tore the article out of the newspaper, folded it up, and quietly slid it into my billfold. Marty Willigan would remain with me for the rest of the season. I just wanted to keep that reminder as a little motivation.

After that day's match, my coach asked me if I would go up a weight class for the next match. I obliged and wrestled an opponent from a school in Pennsylvania, Jake Homiak from Franklin & Marshall. This was very different from the Willigan match. This time, I completely dominated my opponent, winning by pin. I wasn't exhausted this time and felt great.

Just like the day before, the next morning a teammate handed me a newspaper. And just like the day before, I read a quote from my opponent. This time though, my opponent was completely humbled. He said, "I am the team captain. I'm the leader and senior." Then he talked about how strong I was and how technically good I was. He said he thought he could beat me even though he knew I was the defending champion at a lower weight class, but, "He rode me with a pinning combination before he pinned me. I've never been dominated like that before." Everything he said about me was very positive.

Like the day before, I tore that article out, folded it, and slipped it into my billfold. While the purpose of the first article was motivation, this one I kept for a different reason, and the two motives couldn't be further apart. The first guy challenged me with that quote about how it was going to be different between us next time. I wanted to be reminded of that challenge.

The second guy, he didn't challenge me. He built up my confidence. I used this second article as a confidence booster. If I was having a difficult practice, then I'd read these quotes to get back on track. It was also helpful in my life in general; if I was struggling or something was going wrong, I always had those quotes I could pull out and read again. I used these two thin pieces of paper throughout the season for their different purposes. They became part of my life that year, and they did their jobs.

The NCAA wrestling tournament took place that year at Brigham Young University, home of the Cougars. Owned by the Church of Jesus Christ of Latter-day Saints, BYU is nestled in the shadows of the Wasatch Mountains in the northern Utah town of Provo.

Wrestling at the Mormon-owned school offered one very unique challenge for many athletes and fans, due to its ban on caffeinated beverages. There were no Coca-Cola or Pepsi products on campus. There was plenty of root beer, but you could not find a Mountain Dew anywhere.

The tournament took place in BYU's Smith Field House. The inside of the field house was large and dark with a six-hundred-meter track that went around the mats. Most of the mats were located in the central part of the complex, but two additional mats were needed and placed inside a smaller gymnasium located off to the side of the field house.

One of my early matches took place in the small side gym, against a guy from Michigan. As I was walking toward that gym, I noticed there was a large group of people following me. They were there for the entire tournament, but they wanted to see me wrestle. By the time I got to the door of the small gym, the masses were already assembled and just like at Hofstra, I had to make my way to the mat by climbing over people anxious to see me, this kid from Iowa. They soon got to see me do what I do: I pinned my opponent and, afterward, climbed back over the crowd toward the exit. The crowd, however, went wild. They had witnessed what they'd heard about and loved it.

As the tournament moved along, I continued to dominate my way into the finals. On the other side of the tournament bracket was Marty Willigan, the wrestler who had promised, "Next time it would be different," after his loss.

When Willigan and I finally met again at center mat, there was a raucous crowd watching. The official started the match, and the two of us went right after one another. The newspaper article with Willigan's quote, now worn and difficult to actually read and stuck in my locker in the Smith Field House, came into play. I had been carrying that piece of paper in my billfold for months, and it turned out to be helpful in the match. Motivated by Willigan's printed challenge, I was as focused as ever. The outcome of the match was never really in doubt.

It was different this time, all right. Instead of beating him 12 to 1, I pinned him.

The Anatomy of Defeat

People are really fascinated by my losses. That's okay, because no one is more intrigued by my losses than me.

It is no secret who placed second at the NCAA wrestling tournament in 1970 at the 142-pound weight class. Most people who know wrestling know that I lost that match, but many of those same people have no idea who ended my undefeated 181-bout streak in the last match of my college career. It was the University of Washington's Larry Owings who stopped me that March night at Northwestern University in Evanston, Illinois, with the entire sports world watching. Owings beat me 13 to 11, though I later went on to win gold medals at the 1971 World Championships and the 1972 Olympic Games.

Just how I lost my last college match is more complicated than the seven minutes Owings and I were on the mat. The seeds of that lone college loss were actually planted in the spring of 1969. Having achieved everything a wrestler could possibly hope for as a junior at Iowa State, I felt there needed to be another challenge. At the NCAA Championships that year, I won pretty much everything. I won the championship, our team won the championship, I pinned everyone, I won the most pins, and I was named outstanding wrestler, so we pretty much cleaned house. I felt I needed a new challenge to keep me on my toes and keep me motivated.

That year I won in the 137-pound weight class, and a young man named Mike Grant from the University of Oklahoma won at 145, just above me. We both planned on moving up a few pounds because of the coming change in weight classes for the 1970 season: the 137-class would become 142 and 145 would become 150.

I wanted more than just another national championship for my senior campaign. I decided to go up a full weight class in order to face Grant, a fellow NCAA champion. I believed training to face him would keep me extremely motivated to maintain the edge I needed for my best performance. Not everyone was thrilled with the idea, though. My parents didn't like it at all, since they were concerned about maintaining my winning streak. I never thought about a winning streak though: I just wrestled and won.

I moved forward with the plan, and with ten months to prepare, I circled the date of the Oklahoma match on my calendar and started training again with my focus firmly on Grant. It would be my senior year, and having that Grant match looming would keep me in form to remain on top of the wrestling world.

Even though my parents didn't like the idea, my father did something that helped keep me focused on Grant. Our family owned a motorboat and did a lot of fishing. The boat had a bulky and heavy outboard motor that weighed about two hundred pounds. There were no power trim motor lifts back then, so I had to pull the motor up and out of the water when needed, which was often because the back waters of the Mississippi are so shallow. My father named the motor "Grant." All summer long, he would say, "Pull up Grant, pull up Grant!" as I lifted the heavy motor out of the water.

In addition to the off-the-mat motivation and training, I started becoming more active in the international style of wrestling, called freestyle, and eventually competed in it during the off-season for college wrestling. This gave me more mat time and would supposedly help me with my overall wrestling for the future.

Summer quickly turned into fall, and soon wrestling season was underway for the defending national champion Iowa State Cyclones. I remained focused and trained with my sights set solely on that February match with Grant. Shortly before the showdown, word got out that I was going up a weight class to take on the other defending champion. But the publicity, the hostile crowd in Norman, Oklahoma, and Grant knowing about my move to take him on didn't matter: I won the match 9 to 4.

I was happy I won, of course, but I didn't feel that good about the match. Grant took me down once, and that really bothered me. I took a bad shot and he was able to get behind me for the takedown. Still, I had worked toward this match for ten months, and I felt the motivation that got me there worked. But the season was not over yet.

With my match against Grant over, I faced a problem. The Grant match was good in a way because it gave me a higher goal to work toward, but it was bad because my focus was all out of whack. Everything I did that season was for the Grant match. I had focused on it and trained for it, and now there were just six weeks until the NCAA tournament. Preparing for it felt anticlimactic, because for ten months I had not focused on it at all. My mind had been on Grant, and now, with that victory behind me, I didn't quite know what to do. It's difficult to focus on a goal for ten months and peak for that match and then refocus so that you peak again in six weeks. My goal had been beating Grant, but it should have been dominating the NCAA tournament. Grant was a stepping stone along the way.

I didn't realize my focus was off going into the NCAA tournament, but I could tell it was not like the two previous years. My brain wasn't there, even when we arrived at the arena at Northwestern. I took in the atmosphere of the tournament instead of focusing on myself, the team, and our performance. I never fully got that focus back, and that was a problem.

Adding to the madness was the amount of media and attention I was receiving, which was difficult because I'm naturally pretty reserved. A twenty-page pullout from the local newspaper featured me on its cover. Countless members of the media requested interviews, which I granted. And then there was ABC's *Wide World of Sports*. The weekly Sunday afternoon television program was a staple in the 1960s and 1970s before the days of cable television. The program featured different sports and athletes from all over the world, and this particular week, I was their cover boy. They had me tape a commercial, which was never used, where I said, "Watch *Wide World of Sports* and see me finish my high school and college wrestling career undefeated." It was just weird.

In addition, before the tournament even began, I received several honors and awards from various organizations, including being named Wrestling Man of the Year from our national wrestling governing body and being honored by Iowa State University at my last dual match with a blanket that was to say "Undefeated National Champion, Most Pins, Outstanding Wrestler, and so on, at the 1970 NCAAs." It didn't add pressure per se, but it did make focusing on the tournament more difficult.

Then, I did something I didn't normally do. I read an article before the tournament about Owings after he told the media, "I'm going to beat Dan Gable." My teammates thought that I should read it to get fired up. The opposite happened, because I was already off-track, and this allowed Owings to get inside my head. Then during the tournament I watched Owings wrestle. I never did that. I never worried about how someone else wrestled. I always just focused on my own matches.

I ended up meeting Owings in the finals, and as I made my way to the mat for the final wrestling match of my college career, before a nationally televised audience, my mind was not in the right place, and I knew it. As I walked onto the mat, I thought, "I have to watch out for his cradle." That gave me pause, and I tried to get myself back into focus: "What? Watch out for his cradle? What kind of focus is that? That's focusing on him and not on what I'm going to do. It's the wrong kind of focus." I entered the NCAA tournament with a college record of 176 wins and zero losses. I should have been concentrating on winning matches 177, 178, 179, 180, 181, and 182, but I didn't. I focused more on Owings's threatening cradle.

The match began, and Owings went right after me, but I still scored the first takedown. It seemed like everyone watching that night just assumed I would coast to another victory and finish my college career undefeated. This started to slip away though when Owings battled early to take a 7-to-2 lead. I responded in kind, and actually led 10 to 8 with thirty seconds left in the match. But in the end, I, "the unbeatable Dan Gable," lost 13 to 11.

With Owings and his coach celebrating on the mat, I was dejected and stunned. After shaking hands and walking away from the mat, my teammates and my parents offered their support with heartfelt hugs. Others began to join in with the sympathy and condolences, which unnerved me. I didn't want total strangers hugging me and feeling sorry for me, so I took refuge in our team's locker room.

I sat on a bench and tried to figure out what had just happened. I had never lost in high school or college wrestling before, so this was a new and very uncomfortable feeling. The sense of defeat was not just on the surface; it went to the very core of my being. I wasn't sure what to do, except to sit there and think.

I could hear the cheering crowd above from the locker room, but then something else caught my attention: the sound of a running shower. I slowly walked over to the shower, and there stood my teammate, Chuck Jean, the Cyclones's 177-pound wrestler. His own national final was up next, but here he was, showering. I asked him what he was doing.

"Dan, I've never been in the lineup when you've lost, and I'm not about to start now," Jean said. This meant he was planning on forfeiting his national championship.

My depression fled and my healing began. The coach I would someday be came to life. I began yelling. "Chuck! This will hurt me more if you don't go out there and win this match for me, your friend and captain! Get going!"

It was like a light bulb switched on inside him. Jean jumped into his uniform like a firefighter jumping into his jacket and boots. He went back out for his final match and won. Now I could at least go back home with just my loss, not mine and Chuck's. That would have made the tournament more of a nightmare.

The Cyclones won the national team championship that night. When we got back to Ames, about five hundred fans greeted us to celebrate the title. Each member of the team climbed out of the car to great cheering, but when I stepped out, there were a few awkward moments. I wasn't sure how to respond to the fans, and they didn't know how to respond to me. But with my healing already started, thanks to Jean, I was still able to make the most of the moment.

I walked into the building that housed the wrestling room with my still-excited teammates. Everyone wanted to celebrate, except me; I had just one thing on my mind. I asked a couple of my teammates who were still cheering to practice with me. They were nice enough to put off their celebrating for a bit and come help me and allow me to wrestle. It only took an hour before my confidence started returning. I thought, "Wow! I'm still good; nothing is different. I didn't lose my domination in this sport." It was an important step toward my comeback.

There were still hurdles, however, for I was fixated on my loss to Owings. Even worse, I was unable to talk to my biggest fans, my parents. It wasn't that I didn't want to talk to them. But every time

I got on the phone with them, my throat would tighten up, and no sounds would come out.

Early one morning a couple of days later, a knock on the door woke me out of a dead sleep. I made my way to the door, and there stood my mother. She was always an early bird, and she did what only a parent would do to pull her son out of his funk: she drove from Waterloo to Ames to set me straight.

"We have been trying to reach you!" she said.

I stood there, frozen. My throat tightened up, and as hard as I tried, no words came out. When I still didn't say anything, she slapped me in the face. That's all it took, and suddenly I could talk to her again.

My mother came inside, and we spoke for a bit. She knew how to reach me, and she did just that. The first thing she did was tell me that she loved me. The second thing was tell me it was time to get on with the rest of my life. It wasn't a long visit, but she got me talking and reminded me that I was still great and that I had plenty of life to live. It was one of those things only a mom could have done.

After that visit, I knew I had to put an end to the constant sympathy I received everywhere I went. Everyone meant well, but finally I just said, "No more sympathy!" It was time to move on, and I knew it.

But I still wanted real wins, not just the ones I picked with my teammates in practice. Fortunately, I had plenty of reasons to keep training. The NCAA All-Star match, the State of Iowa All-Star match, and the biggest and toughest USA event, the National Freestyle Championships, were all coming up.

I won easily at the first two meets, but the National Freestyle Championships were tough. Owings was in that tournament, but he lost in the early rounds, and I went on to win in fine fashion. I was back on track to my goal of winning the Olympic gold medal. Best of all, I was no longer briefly questioning myself like I had after my loss.

With the month-long emotional rollercoaster behind me, I began intense training, but with a new formula. I would no longer just out-work everyone else. Now I added something new to my training approach. I studied and improved my scoring from standing positions and my defense as well. I did much more analysis of tactics and skills that top performers used in freestyle wrestling. I realized that something had gone wrong in the Owings match and that I needed to spend more time on the details, not just outright hard general work, which I was already doing. I started to train smarter, while continuing to outwork everyone.

The loss became a turning point for me. As I have said many times, I won 181 matches, lost one, and then got good.

Standing in front of our garage, age 4. Courtesy of the Gable family.

Showing off my catch with my parents, Mack and Katie, while on a family fishing trip. Courtesy of the Gable family.

Hanging out with my sister, Diane, on a family fishing trip in Canada. Courtesy of the Gable family.

Proudly displaying my YMCA athletic letter in March of 1958 with my sister, Diane. Courtesy of the Gable family.

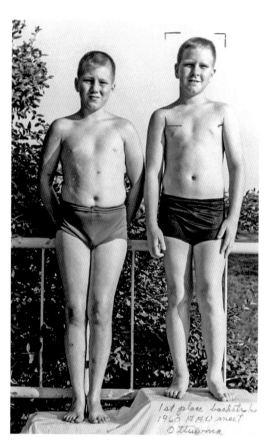

I'm standing on the right, just after I won first place in the backstroke at the 1960 AAU meet in Ottumwa, Iowa. Courtesy of the Gable family.

My sister, Diane Gable, as a teenager. Courtesy of the Gable family.

Me, wrestling Gary Stewart of Cedar Rapids during the state semifinals my sophomore year of high school in March of 1964. My mother noted on the back of this photo that I beat him 7 to 0 in this match. Courtesy of the Gable family.

Me, wrestling in a home dual my sophomore year of high school in 1964. Standing in the background is my sister, Diane, who was murdered only a few months later. Courtesy of the Gable family.

The 1966 Waterloo West High School state champion wrestling team (left to right): Phil Sherburne, Bob Heene, Mike Cowell, Marty Dickey, and me. Marty and I were both seniors this year. Courtesy of the Gable family.

Wrestling with a friend while at home in Waterloo, Iowa. Courtesy of the Gable family.

The entire 1972 US Olympic freestyle wrestling team. Courtesy of the Gable family.

1972 US Olympic freestyle wrestling medalists (left to right): John Peterson, silver medalist; Bill Farrell, coach; Ben Peterson, gold medalist; Wayne Wells, gold medalist; me, gold medalist; Chris Taylor, bronze medalist; Rick Sanders, silver medalist. Courtesy of the Gable family.

My teammate, Rick Sanders, on the podium after winning the silver medal at the 1972 Olympics. Courtesy of the Gable family.

Me, on the podium after winning the gold medal at the 1972 Olympics.
Courtesy of UI Athletics.

Kathy and I at our wedding on May 18, 1974. Courtesy of the Gable family.

Me, with Iowa Head Coach Gary Kurdelmeier while I was his assistant coach. Courtesy of UI Athletics.

Me, with Ed and Lou Banach. Courtesy of UI Athletics.

Kathy cheering on the Hawkeye wrestlers at the 1979 Big Ten Tournament while pregnant with our second daughter, Annie. Courtesy of the Gable family.

I've always had a hard time sitting still while coaching. Courtesy of UI Athletics.

Celebrating another Hawkeye victory. Courtesy of UI Athletics.

Tom Brands in action on the mat. Courtesy of UI Athletics.

Terry Brands taking down his opponent. Courtesy of UI Athletics.

Coaching the Hawkeye wrestlers in 1991.
To the left is Royce Alger and to the right is Jim Zalesky.
Courtesy of the Gable family.

Annie with her friend Courtney Rhoades in front of the Hawkeye bus in Dubuque, Iowa, in 1990. Courtesy of the Gable family.

Mackie on the Hawkeye bus with our dedicated bus driver in Dubuque, Iowa, in 1990. Courtesy of the Gable family.

Lincoln McIlravy dominating his opponent. Courtesy of UI Athletics.

Even after hip surgery, you couldn't slow me down. Courtesy of UI Athletics.

My entire family gathered at my daughter Mackie's wedding in 2013.
Back row (L to R): Molly (holding Louie), Danny, Annie (holding Archie), Mike, Justin, Mackie, Kathy, me, Jenni, Eliza, and Brian.
Front row (L to R): Mickey, Danny, Elsie, Betsy, Gable, and Jake.
Not pictured is my grandson Sammy, who was born a year later.
Courtesy of the Gable family.

Making a Comeback

Fully bouncing back from my loss to Larry Owings in March 1970 was quite a journey. I had to get back to what I did best and assure myself that I was still good. It helped that the NCAA All-Star match, the State of Iowa All-Star match, and the National Freestyle Championships were the first, second, and third weekends after my loss to Owings and that I won all three. I had little time to wallow and feel sorry for myself.

I also knew that I needed to focus on freestyle wrestling, which is the style used in the Olympics and is different from folkstyle, which is used in collegiate wrestling. If I was going to successfully move into this even more competitive field, I needed to get my head in the game.

The summer of 1970 went by quickly. I was an alternate for Bobby Douglas, who retired after that competition with numerous medals to his credit, on the United States' World Championship Team in Edmonton, Canada. I watched the 1970 World Championships like a wolf, knowing I was next. I soaked up everything I could to help me win at this level of competition. It gave me a lot of experience for the future.

After that, 1971 came rapidly. In January and February of that year, the Soviet Union's team went on a tour of the United States to four different cities, and I wrestled against them each time. The US coaches Myron Roderick and Bill Weick insisted upon this, as they wanted exposure for wrestling in general and quick exposure for me. As it turned out, both happened. ABC's *Wide World of Sports* actually featured me on the final stop of their tour. The Russians were winning the team competition, but I quickly gained valuable experience and actually pinned my Russian opponent in the final stop.

I was at Iowa State working as a graduate assistant coach when the 1971 Division I NCAA Wrestling Championships took place at Auburn University. I was there, working out in a room full of wrestlers, when highly respected wrestler and coach Doug Blubaugh approached me and asked if we could work out together. Even though I was successful, there were still those who doubted me as a wrestler, and Doug wanted to get a sense of my abilities for himself. After nearly half an hour of me having a lot of success against him, Doug pulled me aside and gave me a talk. He told me, "Don't ever let anyone tell you that you're not good." That meant so much to me because, at the time, most of wrestling was measured through him.

Next up for me were the Pan-American Games trials and the World trials, both held at the US Naval Academy. I dominated both events, with all pins at the Pan-Am trials and a total score of 50 to 0 at the World Championships trials. This further helped put me back into the right frame of mind.

Training at the Naval Academy was perfect for me. I loved being around so many great wrestlers and being coached by Doug Blubaugh himself. It was Spartan-like, all of us living together in the locker room in bunks. Being around the military and its disciplines really made me feel ready for battle. And I was, just a different type of battle.

Our last few days of training before the Pan-American Games were in Miami, Florida, where we were processed for the international trip. There, we had a small sixteen by sixteen mat inside a hot wrestling room for the whole team. It was difficult, but I loved it.

Running outside in the heat after practice was icing on the cake for me, because it just added to the difficult training.

The 1971 Pan-Am Games were held in Cali, Columbia, and my only tough match was against a Cuban wrestler. Still, I was able to come on strong at the end to win 11 to 2. Because I ran outside every day, I was able to see a little bit of the country. These runs were several miles, but I was there to compete, not sightsee. I was there to do my job, which was to compete extra hard in every match. There, much like the Munich Olympics later, protesters and extremists were making political statements. One Cuban athlete was murdered while we were there, when he was thrown from the high-rise dorm where we were staying.

After the Pan-American Games, we were back at the Naval Academy in Annapolis for more locker-room living and training to prepare for the World Championships. For most of us, these training camps of 1971 went well, but if you weren't truly a wrestling fanatic, they were a little rough. Coach Blubaugh knew a lot about combative wrestling styles and hard running, so that is what we did. It was perfect for me, but not for everyone.

The World Championships were held in Sofia, Bulgaria. The US team was housed on the thirteenth floor, and the building's elevator was broken. Again, this was perfect for me, as the extra workout of climbing those stairs every day was just one more thing that gave me an edge. The competition itself was held in an outdoor stadium. I won the gold medal in the 68-kilogram weight category, beating my Bulgarian opponent in the finals 8 to 3 in front of ten thousand Bulgarians. My teammates also did well. Don Behm won a silver medal in the 57-kilogram category, and Russ Hellickson won a bronze in the 90-kilogram division. It was perfect, or close to it.

I flew home the next day with Russ Hellickson, and we needed to stay overnight in Germany. When I told him that I was planning on going out for a workout the next morning, he looked at me like I was nuts. I told him that I needed to get ready for the Munich Olympics next year. It was at that moment that he knew I was not close to being normal. Still, Hellickson got up with me the next morning to work out. After running a few hard miles, we wrestled on the grass in a nearby park.

My parents didn't travel to the then-Communist Bulgaria for the World Championships and always regretted it. Throughout the meet, my father was constantly at the local newspaper, seated next to the teletype machine waiting for the results. When they finally came across, saying "Dan Gable wins World Title," he ripped off the sheet of paper and took off running through the streets of Waterloo shouting, "My kid is a World Champion!" making people in town ecstatic. When I heard this story later, I loved it.

The summers of 1970 and 1971 were very good for me. They were the first summers where my full-time job was wrestling training. I wasn't making a lot of money like I had with the construction company or the lumberyard, but I was making a good deposit toward a big future payoff.

10

Team USA at the 1972 Munich Olympics

After being beaten in my last collegiate match, I turned things around, got better, stayed focused, and became a dominant world champion in less than eighteen months. My next goal was to dominate in Munich.

Not long after I made the decision to work through a serious knee injury, the spring of 1972 brought warmer days to Iowa. One day, I was sitting outside across the street from my home in Ames, and I had a glass with about two ounces of beer in it. A police officer approached me and fined me twenty-five dollars for having an open container in a public location. I should have just kept quiet, but I became a little mouthy with the officer and was then hit with an additional twenty-five dollar fine.

I figured that would be the end of it, but the incident cost me more than money, as the state newspapers quickly picked up the story. When my father read about it on the front page of the local news, he was not happy. He was so unhappy, in fact, that he came to my hearing and waited for the judge to arrive by his personal parking spot. When the judge did arrive, my father walked right up to him and put a "Think Munich" Olympic support button on the judge's chest. Even though he was upset, Dad remained supportive of me throughout the incident. His move backfired though, as the judge felt threatened. Then my father told him who he was.

"I know who your son is!" the judge said. "Everyone here knows your son. In fact, my son has a poster of him on his bedroom wall."

In the end, I didn't contest the charge, and the fine was dropped from fifty dollars to the original twenty-five. I paid it and learned a valuable lesson about respecting the law. As I've said many times, one needs to work hard in wrestling, but one needs to be smart, too. In this case, the only part of smart was me being a smart mouth, and that doesn't work out well.

When I went to the Olympic Trials, my injured knee felt fine, and I was better prepared than ever. I earned my spot on the team by winning my final two matches by a combined score of 33 to 0, and we set about training. We spent most of our time working out in the University of Minnesota's Williams Arena. It was nice being in Minneapolis because when we had time off, I was able to go back to Waterloo and visit my parents. I often took my Olympic teammates, John and Ben Peterson, with me. The team's 450-pound heavyweight, Chris Taylor, even made the trip to Waterloo once.

Back at home in Waterloo, we had several places to train. I had a twelve by twelve mat in my parents' basement, there was a fourteen by fourteen mat in the basement of my friend Randy Bensing's house, and a barn at a nearby farm had a twenty by thirty mat. There was even a local car dealership that had a forty by forty mat. The barn and car dealership were both owned by Jim Cordes, a close friend of our family. His son, Tony, was a very good wrestler and a close friend. In addition to all that, a couple of local high school wrestling coaches always had a key for their gym for whenever we needed to get in there to train. Everyone knew we were on a mission, and they were looking out for us and supporting us.

Once the US training camps ended and the entire Olympic team was processed in Washington, DC, we were off to Munich. We were able to get a good workout in before we got on the plane, but it was a long flight, so the first thing the Petersons and I did after arriving at the Olympic Village was get in another good workout. After that we got some food and sleep.

We trained for a week before the Olympics started in order to get acclimated to Germany's time difference. When it came time for the opening ceremonies, several members of the freestyle wrestling team did not participate. The word was that being in the opening ceremonies meant being on your feet for five or six hours straight. Since the freestyle wrestling competitions started the very next day, many of us did not want to risk ruining our performance in an event we had all trained a lifetime for. Instead, we watched it on television from the Olympic Village.

The freestyle wrestling event was a five-day competition. That meant five days of weighing in two hours before the competition started. Maintaining our weight was not a problem for most of us, as Coach Bill Farrell had eliminated all of the elements that needed to be mastered ahead of time. Our weights were down, nutrition was high, rules on bedtime and social parameters were in place, and practice times and locations were all set up. This meant the team members could just focus on competing hard. Eliminating any potential issues ahead of time made for better performances with all of us.

The freestyle wrestling competitions were over before the well-known deadly terrorist attack at those Olympic Games. This meant we weren't distracted from our focus on the competition. The attack itself was just one more thing the athletes had to deal with. The Greco-Roman wrestlers competed after the conflict, and I'm sure the attack affected all of the athletes' performances. I know the deadly incident impacted me more over the years than it did at the time. Usually, time heals, but for me the wounds emerged later, after much thought and many reminders.

Our 1972 freestyle team's impact on the world of wrestling has carried on in the years since. Even the announcers, Ken Kraft of

Northwestern University and Frank Gifford, were given credit for their roles in broadcasting, due to the amount of excellent coverage time they received due to our performance. Head Coach Bill Farrell was a successful businessman both before and after the 1972 Olympics, and he stayed close to the sport through his work with Asics shoe and apparel company, until his passing in 2012. It was he who helped sign me to my contract with Asics more than thirty-five years ago. Asics continues, with the leadership of Nick Gallo and Neil Duncan, to be a top sponsor of Olympic wrestling.

1972 UNITED STATES FREESTYLE WRESTLING TEAM

Sergio Gonzales / 105.6 lbs.

> Undefeated in Munich, but was eliminated with three draws due to the Olympic point system.

Jimmy Carr / 114.4 lbs.

> Youngest Olympic wrestler ever at the age of 16. He died in a car crash in 2013.

Rick Sanders / 125.4 lbs.

> Silver Medal. The United States' first world champion, won in 1969. He died in a car crash in 1972.

Gene Davis / 136.4 lbs.

> Bronze Medal at the 1976 Montreal Olympics. Works with Athletes in Action.

Wayne Wells / 162.8 lbs.

> Gold Medal. 1970 World Champion. Today he is a retired attorney in Oklahoma, but is still active in the profession.

John Peterson / 180.4 lbs.

> Silver Medal. Won a Gold Medal at the 1976 Montreal Olympics as well. Works with Athletes in Action.

Ben Peterson / 198 lbs.

> Gold Medal. Won a Silver Medal at the 1976 Montreal Olympics.

Hank Schenk / 220 lbs.

Bronze Medal at the 1969 World Championships.

Chris Taylor / Unlimited.

Bronze Medal. He wrestled professionally for a short time, but passed away at the age of twenty-nine.

COACHES

Head Coach Bill Farrell

New York Athletic Club coach and administrator, along with Asics president of wrestling division until his passing in 2012.

Bill Weick

Longtime legendary Illinois wrestling prep coach. He is a National Wrestling Hall of Fame inductee and is still actively coaching.

Jim Peckham

Successful wrestling coach at Harvard for a decade, and wrestling coach and athletic director at Emerson College for many years. Distinguished Member of the National Wrestling Hall of Fame. Passed away in 2011.

Team Leader Russ Houk

Former wrestling coach at Bloomsburg State College and served as the chairman of the USA Olympic Wrestling committee. Deceased.

The Case of the Missing Medal

I don't always remember what to pick up at the grocery store or the exact time I'm supposed to be somewhere. That's why I'm known for carrying around my date book. Packed with dates, times, names, and phone numbers, along with other notes, the book is a map for me to follow each day.

When it comes to stories of wrestling, though, I have no need for a notebook. My brain is like a computer filled with meets, names, dates, stats, wins, and losses going back to my earliest days at the YMCA, where I was first introduced to the sport that has been my life.

The 1972 Munich Olympics was particularly exciting and memorable. I had won the World Championship the year before in Bulgaria, and that didn't sit well with the Soviet Union. In fact, the Russians were so miffed that, six months before the Olympics, the Soviet Union wrestling officials vowed to find someone in their vast country who could beat me. All this fear and frustration in the international wrestling world for a guy from Waterloo, Iowa.

In the end, I met Ruslan Ashuraliyev, the Soviet groomed to beat me, in the 149.5-pound Olympic finals and beat him 3 to 0. Obviously, I was happy about winning the gold medal, but I was honestly more pleased with the way I competed than with the victory itself. No one scored on me the entire tournament, and the United States freestyle wrestling team had a six-medal finish, more than the experts had anticipated. Still, I was looking beyond this gold medal to the larger picture of the sport: I knew this would help elevate wrestling in the United States. I also knew it meant a great deal to my parents. They were beside me and had watched me train and sacrifice for this goal of winning the Olympics my entire life.

After the final, I stood atop the podium as the gold medal was placed around my neck, and the national anthem played as the United States flag was raised triumphantly. During the national anthem, my mind went into an uncontrollable mode, and my entire life began to flash through my mind. An endless reel of clips from my life played nonstop during that ceremony. However, the most interesting part of the night was yet to come.

After the ceremony was over, I showed off my medal to my family and teammates. We took some team pictures and individual pictures, but then we had to quickly shower at the arena and head back to the Olympic Village. The team and coaches were planning to go out together with parents and fans to eat and celebrate.

As we were heading out after showering though, I discovered I had a big problem: I could not find my gold medal. I thought I had taken it off and put it in my gym bag, which I always had with me for extra dry clothes and running shoes, but it wasn't there. I took everything out of my bag, shook it, even turned it upside down, but nothing came out. Perplexed and a little frustrated, I began asking for help. My teammates and I looked everywhere and even asked the locals if a gold medal that had "68kg" etched in it had been found, but nothing turned up.

Then my mother found out about this dilemma, and it was like having the real Sherlock Holmes working on the case. What was most important to me was how I felt inside about winning the gold medal. I was certain a duplicate could be made, or I could just come back to the next Olympic Games and win another gold medal. I was more upset that I had lost it or that someone had stolen it.

Not my mother, though. She was on a mission. She was going to find this medal, and sure enough, she did. Her search started and finished with my gym bag.

It turned out that the medal had been in there the entire time. The bag had a false bottom, which I had never known about, and the medal was underneath it. I don't think my mother let me have that medal back again for a long time. She held onto it for "safe-keeping."

What is amazing is that you never know what's under those false bottoms. To this day, you wouldn't believe what I have found under those things. I've discovered lots of coin money but only one Olympic gold medal.

12

Olympic Tragedy

I have dealt with both losses and tragedy on more occasions than I care to remember. I experienced them twice at the 1972 Olympics.

The day I won my Olympic gold medal and was carried triumphantly off the mat, my Olympic teammate, Rick Sanders, lost his own gold medal match and walked away unsatisfied with silver. Sanders was a great guy and a great wrestler, but he also liked to party a lot. He often teased me because I was all work and very little play. That was definitely not Sanders. He wasn't mean about things, but I was the butt of many of his wisecracks.

He and I first met in April 1967 at the prestigious AAU National Championships. Sanders was three years older than me, and I had just wrapped up my freshman year at Iowa State. This competition was my first time wrestling freestyle, so I was learning as I was competing. The rules and scoring in freestyle wrestling are different from folkstyle, which is what is wrestled in high school and college. In addition, back in the 1960s, freshmen were not allowed by the NCAA to compete as varsity athletes, so I had battled my way into the semifinals of the tournament. Sanders, on the other hand, was already a multi-NCAA champion and knew his way around freestyle wrestling.

Our first encounter was indicative of how our relationship would play out for years to come. I was standing off by myself getting ready for the semifinals, when all of a sudden I felt a tap on my shoulder. I turned around, and there stood the older Sanders.

"Hey Gable," Sanders said.

"Yeah?"

"You got a baseball bat?"

The odd question threw me off. I was never the kind of wrestler who did much talking, especially with the competition.

"Why?" I asked cautiously.

Sanders quipped, "You better find one and bring it to the semis. You got me next."

This was my introduction to Rick Sanders and freestyle wrestling. Sanders won the match 6 to 0. I gave up four of those points because I exposed my own shoulders. I learned a lot from him that night and started an ever-building relationship.

After the 1972 Olympic freestyle wrestling event was over, the entire team went out for dinner that night. Over the meal, I had a long talk with a disappointed Sanders. He had seen how I had trained and that it ultimately led to gold. Now he wanted to shadow me and prepare for the 1976 Montreal Olympics. He wanted the gold medal he felt he had missed out on.

A major reason for Sanders's interest in working with me had to do with my leadership of the entire Olympic team. I always tried to lead by example through hard work and my ability to remain at a high level of intensity for extended periods of time. Sanders saw the influence my work ethic had on the team, but it wasn't until after the Olympic freestyle wrestling event was over that he admitted it.

I liked Sanders's idea of shadowing me, as I knew it would give me a chance to further develop my leadership skills as much as my wrestling prowess. I was going on to coaching and could direct and guide him for the next four years. I would have been in a position where I could have really helped him prepare for the 1976 games. I wanted him to win the Olympics, too.

Early one morning soon after the competition, I awoke in my room at the Olympic Village to what I thought were firecrackers. Not giving the banging much thought, I rolled over in my dorm bed and went back to sleep. When I awoke again later, it was time to get back to work. The United States Greco-Roman Wrestling Team was scheduled for an early morning training session, and I was going to attend. Taking time off was not an option, even after a major victory. I kept my word to Sanders and went to his room to have him join me.

I knocked on the door, and it took Sanders a little while to answer. It was obvious he had been up late partying. He'd clearly been drinking, and there was a girl in his room. I told him to get dressed, that we were going to train with the Greco team.

Sanders's response set in motion a series of events that changed both our lives. "I'll start tomorrow," he told me.

I was disappointed. I went off alone for two hours of wrestling, while Sanders went back into his room.

Meanwhile, away from the Olympic Village, my parents' eyes were fixed on their television with their phone in hand trying to reach me. As that morning progressed, the world's eyes were on the Munich Olympic Games, but rather than focusing on athletes and sporting events, longtime ABC sportscaster Jim McKay was covering a hard news story.

What I thought were firecrackers going off in the early morning turned out to actually be gunfire, as a Palestinian terrorist group called Black September stormed the dorm next to where the American athletes were staying. The terrorists demanded the release of 234 Palestinians being held in Israel. The Israeli government was unwilling to negotiate with terrorists, so people around the world held their collective breath over the next few days. When it finally ended, a total of eleven Israeli coaches and athletes were killed between the initial attack and a foiled rescue attempt.

When they first heard about the terrorist attack, my parents were frantic. Thanks to the television news, they knew what was going on inside the Olympic Village, but I was so focused on wrestling that I had no idea, and it was going on in the dorm right next to where we were staying. My parents had already lost one of their children to violence, and they were terrified of having that happen again. When my parents were finally able to get a hold of me, that's when I found out about the situation.

I also learned that one of the Israeli athletes who was killed in the attack was the wrestler Eliezer Halfin, in my same weight class of 68 kg. We weren't friends, but I knew him. He was a very good wrestler and a great person. I had a lot of respect for him.

Suddenly, the entire sad situation hit too close to home. With all that was going on, my entire family headed home to Iowa as soon as we were able. I never saw Rick Sanders again.

After Munich, Sanders chose to stick to his earlier plan to hitchhike around Europe for a while. During his trek, Sanders and a driver who picked him up were in a car crash. Sanders, the first American to ever win a gold medal at the Wrestling World Championships, was killed.

Looking back, maybe I should have used a baseball bat that morning in Munich to get Rick to come with me to the Greco practice. Who knows? It may have set in motion a string of events that could have saved his life.

The terrorist attack at the Olympic Games and Sanders's death shortly thereafter have always haunted me. Having experienced real tragedy like that taught me about perspective. Losing my last college match to Larry Owings was devastating. Losing what would have been Iowa's tenth NCAA Championship in 1987 was devastating. But neither was even close to being as devastating as the murder of my sister, the loss of my friend in a car crash, or the murder of Halfin and all of those athletes and coaches that I respected.

13

A New Focus

The first real job I had, as the assistant wrestling coach at the University of Iowa, started not long after the 1972 Olympics. The new head coach at Iowa, Gary Kurdelmeier, was another fine mentor who really helped me grow in my new profession as a coach. Within a month, he turned over all of the practice room training to me, saying, "You're better at this part than me, and the athletes are responding to you, so this is your main area now, and I'll help you learn the other points of coaching." This was a big deal for me, and, yes, I still had a lot to learn about things like recruiting, public speaking, scheduling, and other important parts of coaching.

Early in the summer of 1973, I was somehow talked into wrestling one more match at New York City's Madison Square Garden against the Soviets. It was a good victory, and with that, it was time to move on with coaching and whatever else life offered. Adjusting to coaching, rather than competing myself, was difficult because combative wrestling was still a part of my life. My hours were odd, and I often trained late at night or early in the morning. I had to have that wrestling session, even if it was at two or three in the morning. A ritual is a ritual, and often when the day was done, I'd get one of my wrestling friends and get that workout in, no matter the hour.

Even though my new home was Iowa City and my new roommates were Joe Wells, J Robinson, Jon Marks, Mike Narey, and Matt Clarke, my hometown of Waterloo still felt like home. Therefore, I made many trips home. Waterloo, at the time, was a Mecca for wrestling and provided plenty of action, both on and off the mat. With my life changing, I was becoming more social. When I was home in Waterloo, I frequently went out with old and new friends. After all, in a town where wrestling reigned, there was plenty to celebrate.

With wrestling having been my main attraction for so long, I had not had many romantic relationships. Yes, there was another gender out there, but I had not done much more than notice. I had had a few girlfriends in the past, but those relationships all quickly dissolved, since nothing had ever overtaken my established lifestyle: wrestling training. But then I met Kathy Carpenter, and all of that changed.

Kathy was a senior in high school at Waterloo West when I won the Olympics. The town of Waterloo prepared a massive celebration for my return, which many planned on attending. Unfortunately, due to a storm in New York City, my parents and I were unable to catch our flight home to Waterloo.

"When my girlfriends and I arrived for the planned celebration, the police said it had been canceled," Kathy remembers. "But then we found out Dan and his parents had gotten on a private plane and were going to be landing later at the Waterloo Airport, so we went over there. At the time, he was just Dan Gable. I didn't think in a million years that I'd ever marry him."

Kathy and I officially met at a party during one of my trips home from Iowa City, and we got to know each other through other social events in Waterloo. Our first official date was a simple bike ride the summer of 1973, after Kathy had graduated from high school. It was the simplicity of the date that struck both of us. "We just talked a lot," Kathy says of it now. "We talked about nothing special. We just talked, and we felt comfortable."

After receiving her parents' approval, Kathy, the youngest of ten children, and I began formally courting. Most of our dates that year were at my parents' home, where my mother was always cooking, or at the restaurant that Kathy's father owned. We also spent time at local watering holes with friends, but no matter where we were, we were always together.

The first time we even talked about the possibility of getting married, we were at my parents' house, sitting on the floor watching television. Our engagement became official at the Country Kitchen, a restaurant in Waterloo at the time. I purchased a ring, and we printed an announcement in the local newspapers that the nuptials would take place on June 25, 1974.

Everything was ready for the June 25 date, but then we realized we had to move the wedding. The June date interfered with the US Nationals wrestling tournament. I wasn't wrestling, but several people I wanted in the wedding party and as guests would not have been able to make it. This was the first, and certainly not the last time, that wrestling set the tempo of our lives together.

We moved the date of the wedding up to May 18, but lost two important parts of the event. We wanted to have the reception at the Waterloo Elks Club, and we wanted our favorite band, Milk & Honey, to perform, but both were booked on that date. We were able to secure a different place and band and reminded ourselves that at least all of the people we wanted to be there could be.

Until the wedding, I was still living and working in Iowa City, while Kathy was back in Waterloo working as a teacher's aide at a Catholic school. One weekend while I was up visiting her, we decided to see the horror film *The Exorcist* with another couple. "We were late and got stuck sitting in the second row," Kathy remembers. "I just closed my eyes and plugged my ears through the whole movie, but I could still hear it. It scared me to death!"

To make matters worse, Kathy's bedroom was a lonely room in the basement of her family's house, and the school where she worked was an old building that people claimed was haunted. "Dan would call late after practice," Kathy says, "but because of that movie, I'd call him later because I was so scared." On more than one occasion, I stayed on the phone with Kathy until she drifted off to sleep. I never minded, no matter what time it was.

May 18 came upon us quickly though. The wedding went as planned, and the reception was a lot of fun, even without our first choice of hall or band. We did have one thing at our reception that most people don't get: one of my friends decided to take his clothes off. This was during the streaking craze, but this guy didn't streak, he strolled. He just walked around naked, and little old ladies were getting their pictures taken with him. Kathy's father eventually put a stop to it, but we still joke about it today.

After getting married, Kathy moved down to Iowa City with me. Nothing really changed though, as wrestling and family have always been in the same sentence for us. Forty years later, it's still the same way.

14

The Banach Legacy

Everyone got beat up in the University of Iowa wrestling room in the late 1970s and early 1980s. Everywhere you turned, there was a national champion or All-American on the Iowa team. We also had the guys from the Hawkeye Wrestling Club who had graduated and were there training for the World Championships and the Olympics. Just about everyone in the room wrestled the Iowa style, which meant always going forward, never easing up, and giving 100 percent all the time. The room was brutal, but great.

In the 1979 season, twin brothers Ed and Lou Banach came in and immediately jumped into the frying pan of America's toughest wrestling room. A year later, older brother Steve, who had transferred after two years at Clemson, joined his brothers. With them came an intense, in-your-face style not often found in young men at this stage of the game.

All three brothers credit much of their hard-nosed mentality to their upbringing. The twins and their elder brother were only thirteen months apart in age and were part of a biological family of fourteen children. After a fire destroyed their family's home in the early 1960s, the Banach children were split up and placed in different foster homes to be raised. Steve, Ed, and Lou were all placed with Allen and Stephanie Tooley of Port Jervis, New York, and it is the Tooleys the Banach brothers refer to as their parents today.

The trio got into wrestling at a time when the sport was going through a major change in Port Jervis. A local man named Mark Faller, who had wrestled at Harvard, returned to the town in the early 1970s to build up Port Jervis's wrestling program. Faller's first step was to bring on an assistant coach, Phil Chase. Chase had no wrestling background but was able to develop a youth program that fed into the Port Jervis High School and teach Faller's style of wrestling: win by the rules, be tough, and lose with class and dignity. At the same time, Port Jervis's football coaches were building a program based on a similar philosophy. Together, the four men helped lay the foundations that led to Steve wrestling for Clemson and Iowa, and Ed and Lou being recruited to Iowa.

This philosophy they learned at Port Jervis made the Banachs a perfect fit for Iowa. When I recruited the twins, they knew exactly what was expected of them. Wrestling at Iowa was about wrestling aggressively for the entire match and outworking every other team, and they were comfortable with that.

The coaching staff decided to redshirt Ed and Lou during their freshman year, meaning they could practice with the team but did not compete as countable University of Iowa wrestlers. This allowed them to pick up an extra year of training without the stress of competing on the varsity level. Redshirting didn't mean the Banachs took it easy though. When Ed and Lou came in the wrestling room, they fought tooth and nail. They battled hard every single day in practice, and honestly, they didn't do that great at first. But they were certainly battling.

The Banachs were there to fight for the Hawkeyes, and that goal led the newcomers to train only with the very best Iowa wrestlers. This approach rubbed a few of their teammates the wrong way, but the Banachs stayed the course, even while receiving odd looks and dealing with whispers behind their backs. I had received similar treatment many years earlier as a young, enthusiastic newcomer at Iowa State. Like I had in the mid-1960s at Iowa State, the Banachs remained focused on their goals, ignoring the smirks and comments tossed in their direction.

"I was there to reach my goals to be World and Olympic champion," Ed explains today. "So those were the kinds of guys I worked out with. I didn't much care what people were saying. My brother and I were focused."

"We practiced every day to get better and help others get better," Lou adds. "So we ended up getting along with people and having good relationships. I have nothing bad to say about the guys [at Iowa]."

The Banachs continued to pattern their practice on those who were the very best in the room. In doing so, they competed on a daily basis with some of the best wrestlers in the nation and world. It was exactly why they were Hawkeyes.

"Ed and Lou were never the most technically sound wrestlers," their older brother Steve says. "They were always brutes. They fought, and no matter what was going on, they never backed down and never gave up." With this attitude and their constant hard work though, over time their techniques improved and became very proficient.

As a coach, I never focused solely on finding weaknesses in my athletes and then eliminating them. I tried to do the opposite: find out what a wrestler's strength was, what would be his best way to win matches. Then I would work with that wrestler to further strengthen that area. Ed and Lou were very good upper body wrestlers, so I had them continue to improve upon that, and it worked.

The Banach twins soon began wrestling unattached, which was a way to compete independently. These matches did not count on their Iowa record and did not contribute to the team, but as they began to have success, those in the room who doubted them began to take notice.

If there were any Hawkeyes remaining who didn't believe in the Banachs, Ed was soon ready to show everyone just what he and Lou were made of on the mat. Even those wrestlers who are redshirting usually try out with the team. This led to Ed wrestling Dave Fitzgerald, an excellent 167-pound Hawkeye wrestler.

Ed lost that match by a point, but what I remember the most is that he really wore Fitzgerald down physically. If you had walked into the wrestling room at the end of the match, you would have thought Ed had won. I knew the kind of ribbing Ed and Lou were taking, but after that match, I told them, "Don't worry. You're going to get the last laugh."

It was that dogged, tough attitude in the face of opposition Ed and Lou had while redshirting that was perhaps the reason they were able, a year later as official members of the team, to pull off one of the all-time greatest comebacks known in Iowa wrestling lore, at the 1980 dual meet versus Iowa State.

No team wanted to beat the Hawkeyes more than in-state rival Iowa State. It was Iowa State that had won the NCAA title before my troops had won the last two in a row. The 1980 Cyclones were no slouch team and were not intimidated by the Hawkeyes when we invaded the Hilton Coliseum in Ames that cold winter night. As the evening drew near its end, the home team led overall, 17 to 7, with just three matches remaining in the showdown. The packed ISU crowd loved it; they didn't think there was any way they could lose. Battling the boisterous and hostile atmosphere, the Hawkeyes needed some kind of magic to pull off the meet.

I asked the twins and heavyweight Dean Phinney, our last three wrestlers of the night, if they were ready. They were.

Ed went out to the mat first and faced number one ranked Dave

Allen. During an initial scramble, he caught the Cyclone and pinned him . . . in all of forty-four seconds. This cut ISU's lead to only 17 to 13, and we still had two matches remaining.

Next up was Lou. His opponent, Iowa State's Dave Forsche, took an 8-to-3 lead at first, but Lou knew he could still win. Lou just stood up, turned, and bear-hugged Forsche to his back, pinning him. Lou's heroics pushed the total score to 19 to 17 in Iowa's favor, with just the heavyweights left to battle it out for the winner-takes-all finale.

Phinney battled his opponent hard and won 13 to 5. Iowa picked up four points on a major decision, because he had won by eight points. The three young men did exactly what they had told me they would do.

Final score: Iowa 23, Iowa State 17.

Steve says of that night, "It was classic Iowa wrestling. It was the Iowa way. You never give up, no matter what the situation is. If Coach Gable even noticed you weren't going one hundred percent all of the time, especially in a match, he would let you know how he felt. Coach doesn't say a lot. He doesn't waste words.

"As for that Iowa State match, I was excited and all of us from Iowa were going wild, but I honestly was not surprised because I knew what my brothers and Phinney were like as people and wrestlers. They were not going to back down or give up. They showed the Iowa spirit that night."

The previously excited and confident Iowa State crowd now headed for the exits in stunned silence. None of the Hawkeyes were surprised. We celebrated the come-from-behind victory, but we had known, not thought, that we would come back and win this match all along. The foundations of this thrilling victory were seeded in the Banachs' first year of eligibility, when they were not yet superstars in the sport but were putting in the groundwork to later leave their marks on the wrestling world.

All three Banachs went on to wrestle at the 1984 Olympic Trials in Iowa City, with Ed and Lou earning spots on the team. The twins both won gold medals at the Los Angeles Games that year, and I coached Team USA to seven gold and two silver, while two more Hawkeyes, Randy Lewis (gold) and Barry Davis (silver), competed beside the Banachs.

A fitting end to the story.

Wrestling Writer

When I joined the Iowa Hawkeye coaching staff after winning the gold at the Munich Olympics, people were always coming into the Hawkeye wrestling room. I had received a lot of attention at the Olympics, so there was a lot of press, and people just wanted to talk to me during that time. I always tried to be cordial when they came in and answered their questions.

One day in November of 1972, a man entered the wrestling room while I was putting the Hawkeyes through a workout. He stood off to the side, and I quickly approached, reaching out my hand to introduce myself.

"Hi, I'm Dan Gable."

"Of course you're Dan Gable," said the man. "Everyone in the wrestling world knows you!"

The man's name was John Irving. He explained that he was a wrestler, that he had been a member of the wrestling team at the University of Pittsburgh and the captain of the wrestling team at Phillips Exeter Academy in New Hampshire. He also explained that he was a writer doing graduate studies at the University of Iowa's prestigious Writers' Workshop. Irving and his obvious New England accent intrigued me, especially when he asked if he could work out with the team or club. Realizing he was serious, I asked if he wanted to get changed and work out after practice was over.

Irving changed into his workout gear, and for the next half hour, the two of us wrestled. I immediately liked his style of wrestling. He didn't need more than twenty or thirty minutes of wrestling with short breaks to get a good workout with me. I had already been working out for about an hour when he showed up, but no matter what I threw at him, he would not quit. He was a hard-nosed competitor. He got knocked down a few times, but John always came storming back, and we both enjoyed it.

This was the first day of a long and solid friendship. We connected through our passion for wrestling. We both loved to compete, which made it very easy to respect and get along with him.

Our relationship continued inside and outside the wrestling room when Irving had an idea to combine his time at the Writers' Workshop with his love of wrestling. He asked me if he could follow me around for a while and then write an article about me, and I agreed. Once Irving sold the story idea to *Esquire,* he became my shadow. I was amazed by how much detail he picked up on. He even noticed this weird thing I do, using my index and middle fingers to run my hand along a wall whenever I walk close beside one. I didn't even know I did that, but John was so into details that he picked up on it.

One chilly evening, Irving and I drove the short distance from Iowa City to Solon, Iowa, where I was going to be the main speaker at a high school winter sports banquet. The two of us sat together for dinner, and then I gave my speech. Afterward, they set up a table for me to sign autographs. Irving sat next to me the whole time, scribbling notes as people handed me pieces of paper to sign. Then toward the end, one particular person slid a piece of paper along the table for me to autograph. After I did, they slid that piece of paper over to John. He said, "Oh, you don't want my autograph. I'm nobody." Then he looked right up at this person and added, "But I will be someday." I was surprised by the bold statement but really admired him for his confidence.

Not long after that night, *Esquire* ran his story about me with the title "Gorgeous Dan, The Almost Undefeated Life of the World's Best Wrestler." I really liked the article, and I was impressed all over again by how much detail he had managed to learn about me and my life, just by following me around and watching me.

Of course, John Irving's words to the young fan in Solon during the autograph session proved true, as he was featured on the cover of *Time* just a few years later. His books have since sold millions, and *The Hotel New Hampshire*, *The Cider House Rules*, *The World According to Garp*, *A Prayer for Owen Meany*, and *A Widow for One Year* have all been adapted into movies. Even as his career as a writer exploded, Irving always gave credit to his roots in the sport that brought the two of us together: he has always told me that it was wrestling that gave him the discipline needed to be the writer he has become.

16

Saving Barry Davis

The first sign of trouble came when I did a quick head count.

The Iowa Hawkeyes wrestling team was preparing for our trip to Ann Arbor, Michigan, where the 1982 Big Ten Championships were scheduled to take place. But the morning we were about to leave, one of my wrestlers was missing. Sophomore Barry Davis, a returning All-American and ranked number one in the nation in the 118-pound weight class, was nowhere to be found.

"Where's Barry?" I asked my troops.

I was answered with a bunch of shrugged shoulders, "I don't knows," and blank stares.

I made my way over to Davis's locker and saw a note taped to it. The outside of the note read: "To Coach Gable." I immediately knew this could not be good news as I opened it and read the contents:

Coach Gable: I am sorry I'm not going to make this trip with you guys. I wish you all the very best at the championships. Don't try to find me because you never will. Good luck.
  Barry Davis

In that moment, my first thought was, "Oh, boy . . ." I was worried about Davis and I was worried about the team. In those years, Davis was our spark plug and got the whole team fired up.

Davis was always a character, popular with his teammates and our fans. A few years later, when Iowa would host Oklahoma State, Davis would stand across the mat from his opponent for initial introductions. When the announcer called Davis's name, he would step forward and mime drawing a gun and shooting across the mat at his Oklahoma State Cowboys opponent. Our fans would just go nuts.

That moment may never have happened though, had I, in 1982, standing in front of Davis's locker, not jumped into action. I turned to the team and read the letter aloud, then asked again, "Does anyone know where Barry is?" The locker room was silent except for a dripping shower. I immediately went into problem-solving mode.

I am a big fan of Sherlock Holmes. I used to watch the Sherlock Holmes television program in the 1970s and really admired his theory of deductive reasoning. Basically, when investigating something, you take six possible solutions and reduce them down to the two strongest possibilities. I knew then that I was in a Sherlock Holmes moment; I had to find Davis.

I immediately put together a plan. The assistant coaches would take the nine competing wrestlers and a few alternates to the airport to catch their flight to Detroit, then drive the ninety minutes to Ann Arbor so they could make the 6:00 P.M. weigh-ins. I was going to stay behind in Iowa City and do whatever I could to find Davis. I would meet up with the team later, with or without their teammate.

As the team headed out, I went up to my office. I pulled out a yellow legal pad and pencil and began making a list of all sorts of possibilities as to where Davis could be, including who may have seen him the previous evening. I also called the twenty wrestlers who were not travelling to Ann Arbor to compete to get them involved in searching for Davis. I sent them out into different parts of the community to look for their missing teammate and also interviewed each one to see if they could shed any light on this mystery.

As I made notes and talked to my wrestlers, I had an interesting thought: if Davis had been in the locker room the previous night to tape the note on his locker, the overnight custodial staff may have seen him. It didn't take me long to find the overnight custodial workers, who proved my hunch right. One of them told me that one of my wrestlers had indeed been in there last night. He was in the sauna for a while and then just left around four in the morning.

With that one piece of concrete information, I raced back to my office and continued contacting members of the team. I kept asking questions, coming up with possibilities, and dropping those least likely. Finally, another piece of information came in, this time from a teammate.

One of the guys on the team told me he thought Davis was at a house with some friends. The house was located in a part of Iowa City that I wasn't familiar with, but I was able to start honing in on him. Within an hour, I had more information about where to look, and I headed out there to track him down.

All the while, time continued to move, and I was running out of the time necessary to both find Davis and get us to Ann Arbor before weigh-ins at 6:00 P.M. Undaunted, I drove across town to the area where the house in question was located, while my team members worked feverishly on their own searches.

I had the address of the house where Davis's teammates suspected he was staying, but when I got to the general area, I needed a phone book to figure out where the exact street was located. This was in the days before cell phones and GPS, when phone books all had city maps in them.

I saw a large grocery store ahead and knew they would have at least one pay phone; where there is a pay phone, there is a phone book. I pulled my car into the Hy-Vee parking lot at 7:30 A.M. and went straight into the store, making a beeline for the pay phone located next to the checkout stand. Standing there with two large bags full of groceries was a young man. He was short, with a round but athletic-looking face. It was Barry Davis.

As soon as I saw him, I started to cry. I'm an emotional guy, and here is Barry, whom we've been searching the entire city for, and he's about to quit. He was on the verge of giving up.

■ ■ ■

"I saw Coach Gable and I immediately blurted out, 'I haven't eaten anything,' and I dropped the bags to the floor," Davis, now head wrestling coach at the University of Wisconsin, remembers. "I couldn't believe he had found me."

Today, Barry Davis is open about what led up to his vanishing from the Hawkeye wrestling team on the eve of the Big Ten Championships. In 1982, college wrestling weight classes went in reverse as the season progressed, so that what had started as the 121-pound weight class in November had become the 118-pound class by the end of the season. The constant cutting of weight had simply gotten to him.

"The year of cutting weight just wore on me," Davis says. "I'm a self-motivating kind of guy, and it just got to me. I remember at the end of the season, I was wrestling Kevin Darkus, the number two–ranked guy, and I wasn't even thinking about the match because I was so focused on making weight. That's not how you prepare for a big match or any match."

The day before the Hawkeyes were scheduled to leave for Michigan, Davis felt his entire routine was off. He had a distinct system for making weight, and it didn't seem to be working. With the team leaving for the Big Ten Tournament the day of weigh-ins, Davis decided he would get as much sleep as possible and head over to the work-out facility at 4:00 A.M. to finish making weight.

"It was awful," Davis said. "I was real tired, and I just was not into what I was doing because my routine was off, and I went into the sauna and the weight wasn't coming off. I just hit a breaking point and said, 'That's it.'"

Even though Davis had left the note imploring me not to come looking for him, I did so anyway. When the two of us walked outside the grocery store and sat in my car, there was no tough love or shaming. Rather, I asked the sophomore one question.

"I'll never forget it," Davis says now. "All Coach said was, 'What do you want to do?'"

No pressure, no guilt, just a concerned coach ready to support his nineteen-year-old athlete, no matter what his decision was. The moment lasted just seconds, but for both of us, it seemed like hours.

Davis reports, "I told him I wanted to make weight."

■ ■ ■

With those five words, the rest of the day was set in motion. I took Davis back to the university to pick up his gear, and then we picked up my wife. The three of us quickly caught a plane to Chicago. There, while waiting for our connecting flight to Detroit, and with Davis still needing to make weight, we found a nearby hotel and paid for a room we never saw.

Having been up most of the night, Davis was tired and in a bad mood, but he still had six or seven pounds to lose. Three businessmen sat in that Chicago airport hotel lobby and watched as Davis warmed up, preparing to drop the last of the weight. The men thought it was funny, and one of them commented, "Gee I should be doing that." Frustrated and upset, Davis rushed at them, and I had to grab him by the scruff of his neck and lead him out of the room. The next hour consisted of Davis sprinting up and down hotel hallways with me right on his back. Every time he looked over his shoulder, I would be right there, hounding him on.

Davis did get to Ann Arbor in time for weigh-in, successfully made weight, and ultimately won the Big Ten Championship. What really pleased me though was that Barry wanted to be there and wrestle for himself and his team. He was easily motivated to do the right thing, and that was a sign of a good team and good coaching on the staff's part to help make that happen. It showed that with solid preparation, great things can happen and can even create a little luck.

Still, I remained worried about Davis. After the Big Ten Championship, there was still the NCAA Championship Tournament at Iowa State, the home of the Cyclones and Davis's biggest challenge of the season, number two-ranked Darkus. On the Tuesday before the NCAA tournament, practice had been over for some time, and Davis and I remained the only two left in the training room. I was planning to leave that evening to drive to Ames for early morning meetings the next day. The team would meet me later on Wednesday for weigh-ins.

I asked Davis if he wanted to come to Ames with me that night and meet up with the rest of the team the next day. Davis told me no and that he'd be fine. I had a hunch and went ahead and walked out of the wrestling room. As soon as the door clicked, Davis ran after me.

"I'm going with you tonight!" Davis said.

I responded, "I thought so."

Later that night, I drove to Ames with my wife, two of our four daughters, and Barry Davis. That night we all slept in one room, and the next day, Davis made weight at weigh-in. He went on to win his first NCAA Championship in a thrilling final over Darkus while helping the Hawkeyes to their fifth consecutive NCAA Championship.

"That entire experience changed my life," Davis says now. "Coach Gable didn't give up on me. He could have easily just left me behind and brought our backup. He didn't though. He went to work to find me because he was concerned about a nineteen-year-old kid. With all Coach had done and who he was, he still cared enough about me to find me that morning, get me to the Big Tens, and allowed me to go the day before the NCAA tournament with his family so I could be okay. This is amazing and shows the man—the true man—who Dan Gable is."

Fishing with Jenni

There is a near-famous photograph of my daughter, Jenni Gable Mitchell, taken during a home Iowa Hawkeyes wrestling match. In it, the tiny four-year-old girl is huddled under the chair where I sat coaching the wrestling team to another victory. Jenni always wanted to be close to me, so that's where she sat whenever the Hawkeyes wrestled at Carver-Hawkeye Arena.

"I felt protected under the chair," she says of it today.

Being the eldest of our four daughters, Jenni had certain privileges that her three sisters didn't get to enjoy. In addition to sitting under my chair at meets when she was small, Jenni loved traveling with me to speaking engagements, sometimes flying on private planes to these different events. Going to the big annual Oklahoma State match between the Hawkeyes and Cowboys was really exciting for her. And, of course, there was also getting to go fishing. One of my favorite activities away from the wrestling mat is fishing. Ever since I was a kid growing up in Waterloo, I have fished alone, with friends, and with my daughters. For many years though, it was just with Jenni.

One cool day in May, I took a ten-year-old Jenni out on our johnboat on the backwaters of the Mississippi River near Lansing, Iowa. Our family still has a cabin in the area, and fishing remains a Gable family activity.

The boat was sixteen and a half feet long, with a twenty-five-horsepower Mercury engine. I had to operate it from the rear of the boat, and Jenni sat in the front seat. That day, I was eager to get out to the fishing hole, and I had the boat close to top speed. We had a problem with the steering mechanism, the arm that I used to drive from the back of the boat. It was not adjusted correctly, so I had to hold the arm very tightly to keep the boat straight. Normally this wasn't a problem, but I really should have had it fixed.

Jenni still remembers sitting at the front of the boat that day, enjoying the scenery with the thick trees on either shore and feeling like the most important little girl in the world, being out with her dad. No crowds, no fans, nothing but the pair of us, the water, fishing poles, and a day on the river. Suddenly, the boat cut a sharp right turn, sending Jenni flying off her chair and slamming her little body into the side of the boat.

"I thought my dad was messing around," Jenni recalls.

The boat continued to spin in circles as Jenni tried to collect herself. Looking at the back of the boat, she saw that I was gone and that she was alone in the out-of-control boat spinning in circles. My hand had slipped off the tight steering arm, and before I could reach for it again, the sudden ninety-degree explosive turn threw me thirty feet into the air. I landed in the cold water with no life jacket.

When I came up from under water, wearing heavy clothes and boots, I saw my little girl hanging on inside the spinning boat. I was just a few feet away, but with the boat out of control, I may as well have been back in Iowa City for all the good it would do me. I couldn't get back into the boat, so it was up to Jenni to stop it. I had to yell to her and tell her how to turn the motor to neutral to shut it down. Trying to explain something like this to a ten-year-old under these conditions was scary. Had Jenni made one mistake, she and the boat could have taken off without me down the powerful Mississippi River. As the boat continued to spin around and around, I treaded water and was unable to do anything except yell to my daughter and watch. At first, she almost made the incorrect move of trying to straighten the steering arm instead of twisting the throttle. But then Jenni searched the handle and finally saw the button she needed to hit to shut it down. With the boat in constant movement and her balance unstable, Jenni sat down next to the engine and reached for the button. She was able to put it in neutral and then hit the stop button. The engine shut down almost immediately, spinning slower and slower until it came to stop with white exhaust puffing out into the clear sky.

"My dad was bawling when he got to the boat. He was so upset," Jenni remembers, though she had an entirely different reaction. The little girl who had saved the day burst into laughter as I climbed back into the boat and we hugged. "I think I was trying to comfort my dad because he was so upset. I wanted him to know I was okay and not to worry. I just wanted to go fishing."

Fishing could wait though. I slowly turned the boat around and headed back to the dock. There would be no more fishing until I got the boat fixed.

When I was in the moment, I was so upset that I had no idea how cold I was. The adrenaline had just taken over, and being cold never entered my mind. All I cared about was that Jenni was okay. But it was still early in the season, so the water was very cold, and all of my clothes were soaked. When we got back to the cabin, I finally noticed that I had been shivering the entire time.

As with almost every experience in my life, I came away with a valuable lesson. That day, I learned that I need to practice what I preach. In this case, that meant prevention. It had been my motto for years; I love prevention. I knew that boat needed to be fixed, and I should have had it fixed before we went fishing. I got lucky that day, but I wouldn't have been in that position in the first place if I had taken my own advice about preventing accidents. I'll certainly never forget it again.

18

A Total Life

The day was hot and humid, and the road leading away from Dubuque, Iowa, ran through seemingly endless rolling hills surrounded by cornfields. Mitchell Kelly had everything he owned in a backpack as he stepped out of his mother's car. He could tell by the way she was acting that the greatest adventure of his life was about to begin. His mother had driven him right to the edge of town so that he could hitchhike the ninety miles to Iowa City. "Usually, if we hitchhiked somewhere, we would just start from home, so this made me know it was an important day," Mitch remembers now. Money was tight, and hitchhiking was the cheapest mode of transportation.

Mitch's mother, Pat, was the hardest worker he'd ever known. She put in long hours as a bartender to provide for her seven sons. Even so, it was often difficult to supply more than the absolute necessities of life. Once, when the toilet broke, Pat had to make the decision between buying food for the coming week or having a working toilet. Food won out.

"It wasn't always easy," Mitch remembers, "but my mother instilled in all of us the importance of a hard work ethic. A work ethic is one of the most important things a person can get."

That day just outside Dubuque, Mitch gave his mother a hug and a kiss, turned, held out his "Iowa City" sign, and began his trip toward the University of Iowa. Like Dorothy seeking the Great and Powerful Oz, Mitch wanted to find and be coached by Iowa's legendary wrestling coach. The trip was long, but he was picked up a couple of times, and eventually got a ride into Iowa City. He knew no one in the dorms, but he did have three brothers in the area, so he at least had someone familiar in these unfamiliar surroundings.

Shortly after arriving on campus, Mitch set out to find me. At the time, it was still summer, and we had wrestling camps going on. We were in the old field house, which was hot and sticky, and wrestling mats filled the floor. When he came in, I was in the middle of a wrestling workout, so he just waited and watched. When I went out a side door to sit on the stairs and take a break, Mitch saw his opportunity and took it. He walked right up to me and called me "Mr. Gable," which is probably the last time he called me that, and asked if he could join the team.

"It was bold, and, in hindsight, dumb for me to approach him like that," Mitch says now. "Still, it paid off."

I gave the young man the same respect and attention as I did any other person who wanted to be part of the Hawkeye wrestling program. I asked him a few questions about his wrestling background and told him he'd need to get a physical and come to the first team meeting. That was all it took.

Mitch was a walk-on with the most respected and toughest wrestling program in the country. He, a guy who had never placed at a state tournament, entered a wrestling room filled with national champions, All-Americans, and even Olympians. The experience was as tough for him as one might expect.

"This wrestling room was rough if you were an NCAA champion, so it was really rough if you hadn't even placed in high school at the state tournament like me," Mitch says. "For some reason, Gable really liked wrestling me. I am guessing it was because I was strong and could go all day, but was not real skilled. Therefore, he got a good workout, but didn't risk injury as much."

For several years, Mitch didn't earn a varsity spot on the squad, but he wrestled as hard and as physically as everyone else. Even in the off-season, he never stopped training. He remained focused on doing whatever he could to help Iowa be the best team possible. I had almost immediately taken a liking to Mitch, and I could tell he had what it took to eventually be part of the team and contribute to its success.

After Mitch's freshman year, I took him on a fishing trip to our family's cabin in Lansing, Iowa, and we talked about our childhoods. I told him about the death of my sister, and he talked about growing up in poor circumstances. I really tried to bond with the young man.

One afternoon during the trip, we decided to get in some good running as we went along a hilly road. We took turns driving, while the other ran alongside the car. At first, I drove while Mitch ran, and I kept yelling at him to run faster as we went up a long, steep gravel road. When it was his turn to drive and I ran, he jokingly did the same to me.

The young wrestler may have been a little too anxious about teasing his coach though, and he swerved off the road, but was able to correct himself. I told him to watch the road, but he said, "You don't worry about me, just pick up the pace." Moments later, Mitch drove the car off the road and into a ditch. We had to get a farmer to drag it out. The experience left me annoyed, not so much that the car had landed in a ditch, but because our workout was ruined.

This remains imprinted on Mitch's mind. "The thing I recall most about the situation was Gable was only mad that it interrupted his workout."

■ ■ ■

During his senior year, Mitch finally got his opportunity in the spotlight. I trained all of my wrestlers to always be ready for anything. Mitch was working toward being the starter at the 158-pound weight class, but then Greg Randall, a returning NCAA runner-up and our starter at 142, tore his hamstring. Mitch was at that higher weight class, but he approached me with the idea of dropping down to 142 and taking Randall's spot. I told him that if he could make the weight, the spot was his.

Mitch made the weight.

He won his first match against Oklahoma State, helping the Hawkeyes win, but just a few days away loomed the annual showdown between the nation's two top-ranked programs, Iowa and in-state rival, Iowa State. The match was at a sold-out Carver-Hawkeye Arena and in front of a large television audience. Mitch wrestled Michael Carr.

The battle was epic as Mitch almost immediately jumped out to a commanding 10-to-1 lead in front of a rowdy Hawkeye crowd. He kept Carr on his back for most of the first two periods as my assistants and I, along with the Hawkeye faithful, screamed for the official to call a pin. A pin was never collected, and the match went into the third period. Mitch was exhausted, and Carr battled back with takedown after takedown. But in the end, Mitch, the walk-on, still proved too much for the Cyclone wrestler, winning 15 to 11.

■ ■ ■

When his senior year concluded, the I-Club in Dubuque set up a Mitch Kelly Appreciation Day at the Shot Tower Inn in downtown Dubuque, to honor one of Dubuque's own who helped the Hawkeyes wrestling team by winning matches against Iowa State and Oklahoma State. My wife and I drove Mitch up there. I think we were all expecting around twenty people to show up, but it turned out both sides of the restaurant were full.

"I was surprised, but Gable was *really* surprised," Mitch recalls. "Bruce Babbitt was running for president and was there for dinner.

Someone introduced us, and he asked, 'Is this all for you?' I said, 'Yeah, I guess so.' He then asked, 'Can you take me around and introduce me to your people?' I'm a political junkie, so that was one of the funniest parts of the night to me."

On the way back to Iowa City, Kathy and I gave Mitch a gift: two framed photos of him, a before and after, if you will. The first photo was of him after he threw his Oklahoma State opponent to his back, with me in the background, hand held high. On it I wrote, "Mitch, I can always count on you to come through . . ." The second photo was of the ref at the Iowa State match when he said, "No back points," with me going mad with anger behind him. On that one I wrote, ". . . but we couldn't always count on the refs." Those photos still hang in the den in his home.

Mitch's prowess as a Hawkeye and his childhood poverty remain just the first two acts of his life story, though. After earning his bachelor's degree in psychology, Mitch wanted to continue his education but had to find a way to pay for it. We were able to get him a graduate assistantship. He proved to be a great coach and was able to get his master's degree in social work and then a doctorate in educational psychology.

I never measured an athlete by their accolades when they arrived on campus. I always measured success by what they achieved when they left the program and what they went on to do with their life. With that in mind, Mitchell Kelly is one of the most successful people to ever come through our program.

19

Growing Up (Annie) Gable

Annie Gable Gavin has spent her whole life having people ask her, "What's it like to have Dan Gable as a father?"

"I've always found that to be such a funny question, and one that's so terribly hard to answer," Annie says now as an adult. "The thing is, he's just my dad. I have no one or no other experiences to compare it to, so for me, having Dan Gable as a father is just normal."

As she grew older, Annie started to realize how different her life was from that of her peers. I didn't have a normal job, and even my job as a coach—because many of her friends had parents that coached something—wasn't just a job. It was a lifestyle, and it was our entire family's lifestyle.

I usually dropped the girls off at school in the mornings, and we would all sit together in the front seat of my truck. At moments like that, I always told them, "Look around, look around," meaning "look around at all of us here, squished into this car together." Our family didn't get many moments like this, but when we did, we made sure to make them count. It was important to do so, because after I dropped them all off at school, I would head over to campus for the day and often didn't see them again until their bedtime. Sometimes I didn't even see them until the next morning.

Having their father coach at Iowa for so many years created traditions that other families just didn't have. Our schedule revolved around the university calendar and the wrestling season, which was pretty much year-round, save for a week at spring break and two weeks in the summer. While other families were barbecuing or fishing or golfing with their dads on Father's Day, we always spent the day at Slater Hall checking in campers for the two-week wrestling training camp I ran.

"After that, we would go to Pizza Hut with my dad and his buddies who came to Iowa City every summer to help out at camps. It was what we did every June, and it was a tradition, and it felt normal," Annie recalls.

Most years, we celebrated Thanksgiving with a traditional meal and the annual family turkey hunt. This involved me shooting my gun into a tree, and then all of the kids would run into the woods to find the turkey I had supposedly just shot. "The turkey was always mysteriously frozen and wrapped in a Butterball package and was used for our dinner," Annie remembers fondly.

The day after Thanksgiving, our entire family always left for Madison, Wisconsin, to go to the Northern Open Wrestling Tournament. "Other than Midlands, this was a favorite for my sisters and me. The Howard Johnson's we stayed at had a pool, and the wrestling tournaments were held in an old gymnasium with an ice rink attached," Annie says.

My daughters all enjoyed watching the wrestling, but it was the extras that made this lifestyle so special for them. They even loved the long bus rides, though all for different reasons. Jenni liked to curl up and read a book or watch a movie. Annie liked to socialize in the back with the wrestlers who felt like brothers to her. She loved playing heated games of UNO and feeling like part of a big family. Molly was always occupied by reading and coloring, while Mackie, as the youngest, stayed close to her mother.

"One year when I was still pretty young, maybe eight or nine, my friend's dad died unexpectedly," Annie remembers. "I knew she was struggling and wanted to be there for her and cheer her up. I asked my parents if I could invite her along on the trip. That year just my friend and I got to ride with my dad on the team bus, and we met my mom and sisters up in Madison the next day. We had a great time, and our big extended family of wrestlers seemed to help take her mind off the sadness she was having at home and raised her spirits."

A few days after Christmas every year, our family always traveled to Northwestern University in Evanston, Illinois, for the Midlands wrestling tournament. Most years, we drove our family van and followed the team bus, always stopping at the McDonald's at the DeKalb Oasis. "Now, as adults, we stop there often during trips into Chicago, and every time, I'm taken back to those Midlands trips as a kid. Midlands was my favorite trip because our hotel had an indoor-outdoor pool and a glass elevator. Our hotel was also right across from a mall, so after-Christmas shopping was always on the agenda between wrestling sessions."

The one thing Annie and the other girls didn't like about Midlands was that the hotel we stayed in played a continuous loop of my NCAA finals match from my senior year at Iowa State during the tournament. This was *the* match against Larry Owings, who to Annie as a kid, was the devil himself. "The NCAAs had been at Northwestern University that year, so I guess they considered it their claim to fame and chose to run it every year, over and over. My sisters and I always closed our eyes and covered our ears when we saw it. In all those years, I never once sat and watched the match." Annie had seen pictures and clips over the years but just could not stand to watch it in its entirety or see her father stand in the center of the mat, defeated. "To me, dad just didn't lose, and I wasn't ready to face it."

Iowa's success during the years she was growing up really spoiled Annie and raised her expectations about winning. Anything less than first place felt like complete and utter devastation to her as a little girl. "I remember so clearly the feelings after Iowa placed second in Maryland in 1987, ending Iowa's nine-year win streak," Annie says. "I was only eight years old at the time, and first place was the only thing I had ever known. The congratulations were customary. Our spring break trip taken every year in the week following the national tournament was always happy and celebratory. This feeling of defeat was something new."

Annie still remembers running into the bathroom during an early match of the finals that year. "Jenni and I were both in there with our ears plugged tight and humming our individual drowning-out tunes, when a lady dressed in an Iowa State sweatshirt came in to use the bathroom after our wrestler was pinned by an ISU wrestler, and he had officially clinched the title. Jenni and I were crying."

"What's the big deal?" asked the ISU fan.

"It was like she was saying, 'You're just two little girls, why should you care so much?'" Annie says almost thirty years later. "This wasn't just a sporting event to us. We were devastated because these were our brothers. Their families were our families. Their struggles were our struggles, and we saw everyday our dad's hard work and devotion and it crushed us."

Even to this day, the importance of the success of the Iowa Hawkeyes runs deep in all of my daughters' growing families. If anyone wants to find Annie; her husband, Mike; and their children in mid-March, check the NCAA wrestling tournament. Chances are, that is where they will be.

20

Coaching the Brands

A blizzard raged outside on the campus of Northwestern University in March of 1990. Through the snow, passersby could see a lone figure running wind sprints on the school's football field. If they got a closer look, they would see that the young man wore only a black Iowa wrestling singlet and wrestling shoes. His muscular body gave off steam from the sweat on his shoulders, back, and head. He was breathing deeply as the snow fell around him, but he just kept running. The man was Hawkeye sophomore Tom Brands.

Tom had just lost the Big Ten Championship to Dave Zuniga of Minnesota in a close match. He was so upset, he came right off the mat, stormed out a security door, and just took off running. This was not necessarily an odd response for Brands. He and his twin brother, Terry, who did win a Big Ten Championship that night, both took losing extremely hard.

Tom didn't wrestle a smart match. He knew it and I knew it, but something happened that made a huge difference to Tom personally. After Tom stormed out, a raspy voice called out from near me in the crowd, "Hey, Coach! Coach Gable!" I turned, and there stood one of my best friends, Bob Altmaier, a huge fan of Hawkeye wrestling who had never personally set foot on a mat. "I know why Brands lost," Altmaier said. "He didn't wrestle his style. He didn't attack like he usually does. Tom let Zuniga stay fresh in the match."

It was that simple. Here was a guy who was a fan of the sport but had never wrestled or coached, and even he could see what went wrong with Tom's match.

So while the 1990 Big Ten Tournament went on for another final match, Tom ran. He knew he had to be back inside the arena for his weight class's awards ceremony after this final match or else be disqualified from the Big Ten Tournament and the looming NCAAs. When he reappeared for the ceremony, he was covered with snow and sweat, but still raging inside.

After returning to Iowa City with the team title in hand, I brought Tom into my office. Once there, I told Tom what Altmaier had said and explained that it wasn't as complex as he was making it out to be. I could tell Tom had been overanalyzing the match in his head and was making it too complicated in his own mind. I wasn't trying to embarrass Tom. I knew if I talked to him about his loss, we would see how simple the solution was.

Two weeks later, at the NCAA finals at the University of Maryland, Terry Brands was on the mat battling Nebraska's Jason Kelber. It was a tough match, but Terry won and earned his NCAA Championship. As his twin battled on the mat, Tom prepared for his own final, a rematch with Zuniga. When the time came, Tom ran out to the mat before a wild crowd. This match was different than the Big Ten final. This time, the real Tom Brands was out there, and he attacked and attacked, keeping constant pressure on Zuniga.

With thirty seconds left, both wrestlers went out of bounds. As they went back to the center of the mat, I could tell that Tom looked good, but Zuniga was having a hard time holding his head up. His neck was obviously cramping. The score was deadlocked, but I knew Tom was in a good position to win this match.

Tom took Zuniga down in those final thirty seconds, securing his own NCAA Championship and joining Terry in yet another part of their lives as twins. The brothers were extremely close and shared everything, so when one of the Brands saw the other win, it fired him up to compete. When one of them lost, the other would be angry and knew they had to come through for the other, so they really played off each other well as wrestlers.

Tom and Terry are the only children of Tom (Yogi) and Bonnie Brands. The twins learned early in life the importance of doing everything to the best of their ability. No matter if it was wrestling, school, or any other task, Yogi and Bonnie demanded their sons do their utmost best.

When Terry and Tom were in their early teens, their father had a pile of wood he told them to split. They split the wood but didn't really do a very good job. When their father came home, he was not happy and the boys got in trouble. The next day, when the twins awoke, there was a new pile of wood for them to split, but it was three times larger than the pile the day before. This time, they did the best job possible.

I have always had a rather stern, demanding coaching and mentoring style, which the Brands picked up on before they even became part of the Hawkeye wrestling family. As part of the University of Iowa's recruitment efforts with the two young athletes when they were seniors in high school, they were given tickets to a home football game. As they drove to Iowa for the game, it was snowing fairly heavily. They got in a car accident with a tractor-trailer and ended up in a ditch. Tom and Terry were both fine and were able to get to a truck stop, where they called me. My first concern was for their safety, and when I had made sure they were okay, I asked, "How fast were you going?" When they told me they were going about sixty, I immediately responded with, "The speed limit is fifty-five!"

Other suitors aside from Iowa came calling on the Brands brothers around this time, though. One of the deciding factors for them came, however, during the Big Ten Tournament in Madison, Wisconsin. I had a strong but very competitive friendship with Wisconsin head coach Russ Hellickson, so during one match between wrestlers from our two schools, Hellickson and I began verbally brawling with one another while the Badger fans booed. It got pretty intense, and the whole place started to get unruly. The crowd actually started throwing things onto the mat. Hellickson and I are good friends and have a lot of respect for one other, but we were really going at each other that day. When I finally walked back to our corner, I saw Tom and Terry leaning over the railing of the balcony, their eyes wide open and completely focused on me. That's when I knew they were coming to Iowa.

When they first arrived, the Brands didn't immediately impress too many in the program. Tom and Terry were both getting beat up pretty badly in practice. It wasn't until mid-November of their first year when I knew they were going to be really good. At an early season tourney when I got my first real chance to watch them in competition, I could tell they would be special. Their true form came out in competition, and that's where it counts. For Tom, a match against a very good University of Nebraska wrestler, Terry Cook, showed me I had a lot to look forward to. The thing about the Brands is that they weren't great during practice at first. But when you got them in front of a crowd, under the lights, they were much better. They would attack and maybe sometimes get a little too rough, but our fans loved them. Fans at other schools didn't like them, but they would have loved to love them, had they been one of their own.

In front of others, I never told them to stop being so intense. Behind the scenes, we talked about how to channel their emotions but still keep that intensity. The Brands looked up to Royce Alger, a two-time NCAA champion and world runner-up. Alger was known for pushing the limits of physical wrestling but not crossing the line and getting too rough. He was a master of getting right to that line.

While Tom and Terry may have looked like they were out of control to the outside world, the two young men always lived clean lives. These guys never smoked or drank, ever. Today they're married with families and have always been good men.

One of the twins' favorite memories of their time on the Hawkeye wrestling team came during their very first year. The team was training, and I kept saying, "Okay, this is the last one," by which I meant the last one of a particular exercise, not of the entire practice. One team member became irked and called me out, saying I was not a man of my word. "This guy was real upset," Tom remembers. "Well, Gable kept practice going. He had this case of apples that one of the big wrestling followers, Tommy Thompson, would send to practice each week. So we're wrestling, and Coach took the apples and started tossing them at us. He wasn't throwing them hard or anything, but he just kept tossing these apples and they were rolling around the mat. I just kept wrestling, and these apples were rolling under my feet. I know there was a reason he chose to do that, other than the fact that one teammate may have annoyed him. He was building toughness. A little goofy, but effective."

The Brands twins recognized that, while my methods may have been a bit unusual, I was always trying to help my athletes reach their highest level, not just in wrestling, but in every aspect of their lives. I encouraged them to work at everything with a high level of discipline, whether that be school, social life, family life, or anything else. None of these is more important than the others. They all require that same level of dedication.

Tom and Terry learned these lessons well. In later years, Tom won an Olympic gold medal in 1996 and was the 1993 world champion. Terry, for his part, captured an Olympic bronze medal in 2000 after winning world championships in 1993 and 1995. The brothers are currently the leaders of the Iowa wrestling program, as of 2015, with Tom serving as the head coach, and Terry as the associate head coach.

21

Granny's Powerful Letter

One spring afternoon in 1994, not long after my mother passed away, my wife and I were helping my father move out of the house they had shared for decades in Waterloo. It was a long day as we sorted through many years' worth of stored items, including boxes of letters. My parents kept every letter my father and mother exchanged while he served in the Merchant Marines during World War II, along with every letter we sent each other when I went away to college.

We came across a letter my mother had written when I was home to visit two weekends in a row near the end of my freshman year at Iowa State. Unlike other weekend trips home though, over those two weekends, I rarely, if ever, saw my parents. In the past, I had always been reserved and a bit of a homebody, but now I was surrounded by friends and chose to spend my time staying out very late with them in the evenings and sleeping in during the day. I never called or told my parents where I was or what I was doing. When I was awake and at home, I had managed to close down the once open lines of communication with my parents. I really didn't give them the respect they deserved.

With each late night with no phone call, each brush-off from her son, each day spent sleeping in, and the overall lack of respectful interaction, my mother grew more frustrated and angry. This was not the young man she and my father had raised, and my actions were not going unnoticed. Rather than calling me out on my behavior while I was at home, my mother waited until I had gone back to school during the week and wrote me a letter:

Sunday, May 12, 1967

My Dear Son,

We will now have the mother-son lecture I would have liked to have had during your recent brief stay at our home. We didn't have this due to the fact you were either sleeping, gone, talking on the phone or had company. None of these things I care about except one. The gone one and I really mean gone.

You have always been a good kid (I think). Naturally, I am a little prejudiced, but I can't see too many of your faults as being important. Although I can see no reason for you mouthing off or lying when you're asked a civil question that could be answered with a civil answer. Such as "where have you been?" or "what time did you come home?" not that anyone was snooping—they just cared about it and wanted to know.

I know you are over 18 and think you know all the answers but I am 40 and know you don't know all the answers.

The past two weekends of your behavior have been to the point that you really must think you're something else. You have a very good future ahead of you which you must remember so when you get 40 years you really have all the answers.

You have done a real terrific job so far. Everyone has a lot of respect for you, not only as a wrestler, but as a person. Don't let these kinds of weekends spoil or change people's minds about you. It has taken you just a few years to get this respect, something some people never get in their lifetime. Don't ruin all you have worked so hard for.

I, of all people, want you to enjoy life and have a good time, but I will not condone your conduct of the past two weekends. It is very disgusting and I'm sure you know lots of kids that go out and don't have to stay out all night to have a good time, and if they did they would have to answer to someone, if anyone cared. Maybe when you turn 19 you will find the rest of your life and you will answer to someone—you start with your parents, teachers, girlfriends, wife, bosses, and anyone in your life that cares about you.

Well, this should about clear up my feelings. I know you know I wouldn't bother about what you were doing if I didn't care about you. There is a lot of things I could write that I know that went on during these past two weekends but I know you already know so I don't need to tell you. So I'll close.

Love,

Ye Ole Lady

I got mail from home almost on a daily basis my freshman year of college, and I always looked forward to those letters. Most of them were short, but they always energized me. This letter was shocking, however.

My initial reaction was to crumple it up and toss it in the garbage can. The letter lay in that garbage can for less than half an hour, though, before I pulled it back out and flattened it out as well as I could. I knew that I needed to respond to the letter, which was difficult, but it was something that had to be done.

I called my mother, full of remorse, and tried to use my listening skills to really hear her out. It was a tough call, but it eased my mind, and probably hers as well. Once that was over, I felt better, but that letter impacted many of my future actions.

That letter was all it took for me to snap out of my selfish attitude and return to being the young man my mother knew. I was embarrassed, and it bothered me that I had hurt my mother. She always knew what I needed to hear and how and when to say it.

When we found the letter years later at my parents' house, my wife Kathy read it and explained it this way: "This letter was a way to nip the problem in the bud."

While it was decades old, Kathy recognized that its words of wisdom were timeless. At the time, our oldest daughter, Jenni, was about to graduate from high school. Kathy came up with an idea to utilize the words of Granny. All four of our daughters were very close to my parents. They were their only grandchildren, and they showered the girls with attention. Kathy knew the letter would give the girls good, solid advice from Granny, even though she wasn't there in person, so when each girl graduated from high school, we put a copy of the letter in their graduation card. As Kathy said, "It is a piece on how to act and how not to act."

For my oldest daughter, Jenni, the letter helped reinforce values Kathy and I had done our best to instill in her. "I feel like I've always been pretty respectful to my parents and others," Jenni said of it recently. "Now, as a parent myself, the letter helps me understand that if my children shut me out like my father had done, and led to Granny writing that letter, I would always do something to get the communication going again. No matter what, I would never give up, ever. The letter is always there in the back of my mind."

22

The Tattoos of Chad Zaputil

I first saw Chad Zaputil at a freestyle wrestling practice in Iowa. It was a typical hot, sweaty room full of young athletes working on fine-tuning their wrestling skills, but Zaputil's
aggressive style, strength, and slick moves caught my eye. I also
knew that the Zaputil family had a reputation for strong values and
commitment—something that is sometimes missing in families and
can cause issues for young wrestlers, for all people for that matter.
Add to this his academic prowess, and I knew he would be a solid,
safe recruit—a perfect fit for the Hawkeye wrestling program.

For Zaputil, who was still in high school and visiting Iowa on a
recruitment trip, it was, he says, "A dream come true. I was getting
recruited and I had five official trips lined up. Iowa was the fourth.
I cancelled the fifth. I knew that was where I wanted to go."

Like most Iowa wrestlers, Zaputil redshirted his first year in Iowa
City. He fully burst on the scene his sophomore year, winning his
first of three consecutive Big Ten Championships in the 118-pound
weight class. At the 1991 NCAA Championships, Zaputil fought his
way into the finals, where he met Penn State's Jeff Prescott, already
an All-American. Zaputil didn't wrestle very well in that match. He
didn't represent himself the way he could, and he knew that. As a
result, Prescott got the better of him.

I didn't see Zaputil for a couple of weeks after the NCAA Championships. When I did see him again, I noticed that on his thigh there was now a tattoo of Iowa's mascot, Herky the Hawk, wearing a wrestling singlet. The tattoo intrigued me and I asked him why he had it done.

"I'm going to win it all next year," Zaputil said.

There was more to that tattoo than a reminder of a goal, though. Many Iowa wrestlers had a Herky the Hawk tattoo. When wrestlers come to Iowa to wrestle, they become part of a family. They live together, eat together, practice together, and travel together. It's a brotherhood. That tattoo represented the love and loyalty these young men had for the team. They came to Iowa to be national champions, both individually and as a team.

Zaputil's training increased, spring turned into summer, then quickly back to fall, and his junior wrestling season began. Even more determined than before, Zaputil blasted out of the gate and enjoyed a dominant season. He won another Big Ten Championship, and then at the NCAA Championships, he battled back to the finals, where he once again met Prescott. Prescott came out the victor again, by a single point. Still, a loss is a loss, especially when it is to the same opponent.

"I was angry," Zaputil says of it now. "I never wrestle to get second place. No one at Iowa does, so losing again to Prescott hurt that much more."

A few weeks after the 1992 NCAA Championships, I saw Chad without his shirt on and couldn't believe the new tattoo he had. It was a large hawk with its wings and talons spread out over Zaputil's heart. Before I could say anything beyond "Holy cow," Zaputil looked me in the eyes and vowed, "I will not give up. I am going to win it next year."

The 1993 season was similar to the previous two, with Zaputil tearing through all of his matches. Another Big Ten Championship and a dominant performance at the NCAA tournament led to his third consecutive trip to the finals. His opponent this year was

Clemson's Sammie Henson, a tough, quick wrestler, but one whom Zaputil had beaten earlier in his career.

Both wrestlers competed at a frenzied pace, and in the third period they were tied 2 to 2, as Zaputil rode Henson. Midway through the period, Henson earned a one-point escape, and the crowd roared. The battle continued as Zaputil worked for a take-down, but time ran out. Henson leapt into the air with his arms raised in victory, while Zaputil bent over covering his face in defeat.

Chad had beaten Henson before, but Henson was a truly great wrestler. He actually went on and won another NCAA Championship, and later became a world champion. That didn't matter at the time, of course. Chad had lost in the finals again and that devastated him.

Zaputil shook hands with his opponent and then bolted off the mat, past me, and out the door into the cold night air. We actually had to send someone to find him. We had one match before they awarded Chad's weight class. If he wasn't there to accept it, he would have forfeited the tournament, and we would have lost his team points, too.

Zaputil did make it back in time for the awards ceremony, and Iowa won another team title. Upon returning to Iowa City, Zaputil all but disappeared. I couldn't find him, and my calls to him went unanswered. "I was down on myself," Zaputil remembers. "I had things planned for spring break, and I didn't go. Maybe I was sulking a bit, but it's a tough thing when you work your whole life for something, and on three occasions, you're right there, but you don't achieve the goal. It weighs on you, or it did on me."

With each passing day, I became more and more concerned. Finally, after about three weeks, I decided enough was enough. I basically staked out Chad's house and waited until he came home. I wanted to make sure he was okay. I had also heard a disturbing rumor about a new tattoo, and I needed to find out if it was true.

When Zaputil did finally come home, I approached the house and knocked loudly. There was no answer. I shouted, "Chad! I know you're in there! Let's talk!"

"What do you want?" Zaputil said from the other side of the closed door.

"I'm concerned about you," I told him. "I want to see how you're doing."

The door slowly opened. Zaputil stood face to face with me, saying nothing. "Show me the hawk on your chest," I ordered.

"No."

I reached out and ripped Zaputil's shirt open, and there was the image I had heard about from other members of the team. On his chest, the hawk that had been tattooed there the year before had been turned into a hawk with its massive talons ripping out Zaputil's heart. I gasped.

That was toughest thing I ever saw in my coaching career. I was in shock. I asked myself, "Is this what I'm doing for kids?" Yeah, college wrestling is serious business, but this kid had a tattoo of his heart being ripped out. That's not going away. He got his heart ripped out by Iowa wrestling. Seeing that was really rough on me.

"Losing that last time ripped my heart out," Zaputil says now. "That's what the tattoo showed. You know, that experience ultimately made me stronger."

This experience dampened our relationship initially, but like most things, over time the emotionally wounded wrestler and I came to terms with what happened on the mat over those five years Zaputil was on the Iowa wrestling team. After he graduated, I hired Chad as a contractor to build the cabin in my backyard that I use as an office and workout area. When that was done, he told me he was moving to California, and he's been there ever since.

Zaputil had been raised in a town of five hundred people where everyone knows everything about everyone. Everywhere he went, people knew him. Later on, Chad and his wife were on vacation in Cancun. "We saw a guy with an Iowa wrestling shirt and he approached us. This guy knew everything about me. I had to get away from that kind of situation," he says. After wrestling for Iowa and being in that public spotlight, he sought privacy. He likes living in Long Beach, California, where he is just one out of millions of people.

As the years passed, I remained concerned about Zaputil and how his career was going, though by nearly any standards, he was doing spectacularly. At one point, we met up at a hotel where I was staying. We sat talking in a hot tub and Zaputil wore a T-shirt. I thought he was hiding something and finally asked him why he didn't take his shirt off.

Zaputil shook his head and didn't respond, but I pressed the issue and finally, in a joking manner, lifted the shirt up. There was a new tattoo there. The hawk ripping out Zaputil's heart was gone. In its place were hawk feathers running from his back, over his shoulders, and down his chest.

"It took a long time, but I moved on," Zaputil says now. "I own a successful business, and much of what I learned from Coach Gable I still use in my life today. The time people were at Iowa wasn't all about wrestling. For me, one of the biggest lessons I learned was the meaning of dependability. Coach helped me understand that the little things make all the difference."

23

Molly's Victory

It began with Roger Bannister. I was a big fan of the man who broke the four-minute-mile barrier. Bannister did so in the face of nearly the entire world, including the medical community, who screamed that such a feat could never be achieved. Doctors said it could not be done, that the human body was not capable of pushing itself to the point of running that fast. They said a man would die first.

After Bannister broke the four-minute barrier, that impossible achievement, he collapsed upon crossing the finish line. His body had given everything it had and just gave out. That is what I found really inspiring: pushing oneself so hard that you have nothing left to give. I strove to be like that.

Bannister's moment of collapse after his great achievement inspired my ethic of outworking everyone else and living a strict life of discipline, yet still having respect for others and myself. I always wanted to be at practice, and I wanted to literally work myself so hard that my body collapsed. Not to the point of danger or anything, but I just wanted to push myself as hard as Bannister did.

My ultimate goal was to be in the wrestling room with the team, pushing myself harder than anyone else, and finally collapsing. I didn't want drama, I just truly wanted to reach that breaking point, to be on the floor unconscious and unable to move. I even went so far as to tell my coaches that I may push my body to complete exhaustion and pass out . . . just in case. I felt like I could really do it someday, and I didn't want them to be worried. I wanted them to know that if it happened, to just drag me to the showers, turn on the cold water, hydrate me, and get me back out there.

Unlike Bannister though, I never did collapse from exhaustion during practice or competition, and that fact still bothers me. It shows that there was always more I could have done when I was training. I was always the first one in the room, the last one to leave, and the hardest worker in there, but every day, I would walk out of the wrestling room on my own two feet, look back, and realize I had not reached my goal. I'd always end up going back in and doing another fifteen to twenty minutes of good, quality work, either on my own or, if there were people hanging around, I'd grab them for some more wrestling. If I had needed to be carried out, I wouldn't have had to do that extra work, but it never happened. What it did do for me, though, is give me all that extra time to work out and improve. If you add it up, all of those years of training an extra fifteen or twenty minutes a day, it makes a big difference in the long run.

It also had a profound mental impact on me. When I was on the mat, I always knew I had trained longer, harder, and with more intensity than my opponent. That kind of mental advantage can't be ignored or discounted.

As my life went on, my connection to track and my admiration for Bannister remained. I married Kathy, and we had four beautiful and self-motivated daughters. When any of my four daughters competed in sports, I was not one of those loud screaming parents. Instead, I became privately emotional: I just cried when the girls competed. I was just so proud of them, and I knew how hard it was to compete. My second youngest, Molly, became a good distance runner for City High School in Iowa City. She was driven, and I saw a lot of myself in her and her approach to winning.

In 2000 our entire family learned just how hard Molly could push herself. As a member of her high school's 4x800-meter relay team, Molly was just seconds off from helping her team qualify for the prestigious Drake Relays. With the season coming to an end, and only a few more regular meets on the horizon, this would be Molly's last real chance to hit the time needed to help her team qualify, but there was a problem . . . a big problem: the 2000 Olympic wrestling qualifiers were scheduled for the same weekend in Las Vegas, Nevada, one thousand miles away.

Molly came to me and told me she wanted to stay home while the rest of us went to Las Vegas so she could compete in this meet. We talked about it, and one of the questions I had was why she felt this particular upcoming race could help her make the time needed to qualify with her teammates for the 4x800 relay. She needed to take two or three seconds off of her time, and that's a lot in an 800-meter.

She told me, "Dad, one of the best runners in the state will be at this race. I'm going to keep up with her, and that will definitely make it so I can knock those seconds off my time."

I noticed how Molly said she *was* going to keep up with one of the state's best, not *try* to keep up. I could appreciate my daughter's desire and her plan to achieve her goal. Her sheer determination to help her teammates achieve their goal of qualifying to compete at the Drake Relays was very apparent. I told her I thought it was a great idea and that she had my support. But there was still the logistical problem of staying behind in Iowa City while the rest of the family went with me to cheer on the wrestlers in Las Vegas. That part of the decision needed to be made by the real authority in the home: Kathy.

After talking with her mother, Molly was given the green light to stay home and chase after her dream, with the hopes of her teammates resting on the event. This agreement included Molly staying with a family we knew and trusted and having someone in the stands at the meet with a cell phone to talk us through the race.

The day of the race, we were at the Olympic qualifiers. At one point, there was a break in the action, so I walked over to the stands where my family was sitting, and my wife quickly announced, "Hey, the race is about to start." She was on the phone with one of Molly's friends, Eliza, who was all set to deliver the play-by-play, which Kathy then repeated to the rest of the family.

"The gun has gone off, and the race has started!"

I started to pace and began sweating. Yes, the Olympic qualifiers were right in front of me, but at that moment, my thoughts and focus were in Iowa with Molly. I envisioned my daughter on the track, focused on her goal, as she made her way around the track twice for the 800-meter race.

"Molly's staying right up with that top runner!"

I was impressed but remained logical. Even though the 800-meter is a relatively short race, it is still two big laps.

"They finished the first lap, and Molly's right up in the front. She's right on the heels of that top runner, and she's pulled ahead of everyone else."

Not only was Molly racing against a highly touted runner, but after the first four hundred meters, she was well ahead of the time she would need to qualify for the Drake Relays. Still, as was customary when Molly competed, I could feel my blood pressure and sense of anxiety increase. It was brutal because I could see it clearly in my mind. I knew how hard she must be running and how exciting the race was, with Molly pushing one of the state's best 800-meter runners. My nerves and excitement reached their boiling point as we waited for more news.

"There's two hundred meters to go and Molly's still with the leader! She's doing a great job! I can hear the crowd cheering, 'Go, Molly, go!'"

My heart raced even more, my breathing increased, and sweat began to roll down my forehead as I paced.

"There's only one hundred meters to go, and Molly's pulled up even with the leader! She might win!"

I hung on every word, envisioning Molly gritting her teeth and pumping her arms, expending every ounce of energy and mental power she had as she raced toward the finish line. I waited and looked expectantly at Kathy.

Then suddenly, she said, "The cell's dead."

My heart sank. What was going on back in Iowa? Kathy scrambled to reconnect with Eliza. She even hit the phone, in case there was a loose wire. As Kathy tried to reconnect, I paced the floor of the arena, sweating and running my hands through my hair one moment and folding my arms the next. Seconds passed. The race would have been over by then, and I knew it, but I didn't know what had happened in those last closing moments.

Finally, the phone reconnected with Eliza. Kathy listened intently, and the look on her face said volumes. I knew something was not right.

We had lost our connection because Eliza had put down her phone and raced down to the track. Molly had collapsed two yards from the finish line. Kathy's eyes welled with tears. We both felt the anguish of being so far away when we knew Molly needed us.

In the end, Molly was fine, and though she did not win the race or qualify for that race at the Drake Relays, in my eyes her arm was raised in victory. She did something I could never do: she went to the very end of all she had, pushed herself to the point of total exhaustion. That is how much she wanted to succeed for herself and for her teammates. I could not have been more proud.

Ace in the Making

I want to tell you a story about Lincoln McIlravy. Rather, I want to tell you a story that is as much about McIlravy as it is about what went on around him as a freshman wrestler at Iowa.

McIlravy came into Iowa's wrestling program for the 1993 season. He was unusual in that he was a *five*-time state wrestling champion from South Dakota. He was also one of about three guys in all my years at Iowa who was able to come in from high school and compete in our wrestling room right away. Competing in that room right out of high school was brutal, but Lincoln did it.

We made the decision early in the year to have McIlravy redshirt during his freshman year, giving him the chance to wrestle with the team without losing any eligibility. The Hawkeyes were already a strong team that season and were eyeing a third consecutive, and fourteenth overall, NCAA Championship. The pieces were in place for another title run, and the Hawkeyes were strong right out of the gate. Still, we were always looking ahead and planning long-term. We wanted to give McIlravy the chance to build to his fullest potential and possibly lead the team in future years.

However, when the season entered its second half, and the frigid winter winds whipped through Iowa City, the Iowa wrestling team hit a cold patch of its own. The two-time NCAA champions entered a slump that included a 24-to-20 loss to Nebraska and the emergence of Penn State as serious competition. This was the first year

Penn State competed in the Big Ten, and they were very good. In fact, they were strong enough to potentially beat us in the Big Tens and NCAAs.

I knew that we needed to do something to bolster our lineup. As a coach, I was on high alert. We were back on a national championship winning streak, and the NCAA finals were going to be at Iowa State this year. With the duals season having just four weeks left, I floated a rather bold idea: to pull McIlravy away from his redshirt season and add him to the official team. Doing this meant he would lose his redshirt season very late in the year, but we coaches knew he could be the spark we needed to help us get the Big Ten and NCAA titles.

McIlravy was already proving himself as a redshirt wrestler. The freshman had a record of many wins and a couple of losses against much of the same competition the Hawkeyes had seen throughout the season. Growing up on thousands of acres of land in South Dakota gave Lincoln an attitude of confidence with no limitations. In fact, in practice we had to corral him a bit every now and then, but for the most part we'd let him go. Being from South Dakota, he fit right in with the Steiner brothers, a couple of our best wrestlers from North Dakota.

So with the coaches and McIlravy onboard, I presented this plan to the team. Everyone, including the Steiner brothers, agreed. The senior twins were integral to making this work: Troy Steiner was the defending NCAA champion at 142 pounds, while Terry was the defending All-American at 150 pounds. In order to add McIlravy to the team, Troy would have to drop to 134 pounds, so that McIlravy could move into the 142 spot. The Steiners were willing to make the sacrifice to give Iowa that needed shot in the arm to make us a much stronger team. Still, there was one person who was not happy about the move: McIlravy's father, Ken.

The elder McIlravy wasn't too sure about flushing a valuable redshirt season down the toilet with less than a month left in the season. Doing so brought an eligibility problem for his son. By dropping the redshirt status, McIlravy's freshman eligibility would be used up, even if he only wrestled one match officially representing the Hawkeyes. In addition, if our idea failed, Lincoln, like any wrestler, could suffer mentally and may never fully bounce back. Wrestling is an extremely mental sport, and the difference between winning and losing is often a very fine line. Most matches are won or lost even before they are wrestled. While I completely understood Ken wanting to watch out for the best interests of his son, with everyone else ready to make the move, I went ahead and pulled the trigger.

I believe that sometimes people get stuck in a decision they've made. They see later that there was a better option, but they feel obligated to stick with their first choice because they made that choice. In business or sports, the right answer can change over time. It's not always found in the first sight or the second sight. It's in the consistent sight that you see the right decision. That said, if you're considering a second or third change, it won't necessarily be a better decision. I knew this change with the team had to be made, so I did it, even if Ken McIlravy wasn't thrilled about it.

My next decision was, in some ways, even more important than the first. Now that he was a fully fledged Hawkeye, I had to carefully choose when and where McIlravy would wrestle his first varsity match. I was very deliberate with this entire move, so I wanted to make sure it would be a match I knew McIlravy would win. We were scheduled to face Northwestern University in a couple of weeks, and their 142-pound wrestler didn't appear to be too tough. I decided that it would be the Northwestern match at Carver-Hawkeye where Lincoln McIlravy would make his debut. It would be a cinch. At least, that's what we all thought.

Everything was set. We were all excited, though Mr. McIlravy was still not happy, so it was extremely important that we get Lincoln out there and get the easy win against this Northwestern guy. As the two teams stood across from one another for introductions, there was a definite buzz in the crowd. For the first time, the fans were getting to see this young man they had heard about. Then the wheels came off the truck.

Something happened that none of us were prepared for or anticipated: during the introductions, our announcer had created a special introduction for McIlravy without our knowledge. When it was the freshman's turn to be introduced, the announcer yelled into the microphone, "In his first time wearing an Iowa uniform, from Phillip, South Dakota, Lincoln 'the Dakota Destroyer' McIlravy!"

As a humble young man in his first time at the electric Carver-Hawkeye Arena, the nickname threw McIlravy for a loop. I could see it in his eyes and was immediately concerned. He is not the kind of person who was going to feel comfortable with that kind of introduction. That sort of thing is for guys who have proven themselves and are maybe a bit cocky. Lincoln McIlravy was neither.

The emotional shock of the introduction, along with my own underestimation of the Northwestern wrestler, led to a disastrous first match for McIlravy. After the first minute of the match, he hit an emotional and physical wall. The match could not have gone any worse, as McIlravy dropped a major decision in front of the home crowd, including his family. I knew this was going to be a big problem. Lincoln was so upset I almost had to carry him off the mat. Plus, I knew his father was going to be really mad.

Making the situation even worse was that I had very little time to figure out how to deal with Mr. McIlravy. After home matches, the Hawkeyes always have a party. I knew the elder McIlravy was going to be there, and I knew he was going to be angry. So I did the only thing I could think of: strike first.

When I got to the party, Mr. McIlravy was outside the door waiting for me. I wanted to meet with him on my terms, instead of his, so I went in through another door. When I was ready, I walked up behind him and tapped him on the shoulder. I immediately began talking real fast so he couldn't get a word in. I told him, "Well, that match is over. Now we're just going to have to figure out how to move on from here. No turning back now. Lincoln is committed, we're all committed, and we just have to figure it out together, and I will need your help."

Mr. McIlravy just stood in silence. Since I had taken a positive first step, his emotions were defused. I'm glad I spoke first, because if he had come at me, it would have been ugly. But after I pointed out that we all had no other choice but to help Lincoln get better, he said, "Well, yeah," and left it at that.

Now we all had to deal with the cold reality that the Hawkeyes had a home match against Arizona State and a visit to Iowa State remaining on the schedule before the Big Ten and NCAA Championships. McIlravy was 0 and 1 as a Hawkeye with a major decision loss at the hands of the guy I had handpicked for him to wrestle. We had to figure out how to get this freshman wrestler prepared for the upcoming tournaments in a matter of weeks. It was time to make another decision, but I had another big plan.

We did something that most wrestling teams couldn't have done: we were going to give McIlravy three match experiences in Carver-Hawkeye Arena in the next week of practice. I knew this was a difficult task, but I was determined to make it happen and went to work.

We talked with the basketball team and found out when they didn't have practice and when the floor would be available. Next, we worked with the facilities people and athletic director to set up three match environments between Monday and Thursday that week in Carver-Hawkeye to get McIlravy ready. We knew he needed multiple, real match-like experiences to get him prepared quickly.

That coming Sunday he had a tough Arizona State opponent coming to town, and another loss would be extremely difficult at this point in time, both for him and for the team.

Still, I knew just wrestling inside Carver-Hawkeye Arena in mock matches wouldn't be enough. There needed to be introductions, music, and, most of all, fans. Fortunately, this was Iowa, and this was the Hawkeye wrestling team. Once we got the schedule set, we got the word out through the newspaper to our fans in our community that Lincoln McIlravy needed some help.

The plan worked, as more than two thousand fans came to each match. With the lights down and the spotlight shining, McIlravy was introduced. He ran out from the tunnel to rousing cheers, loud music, and an opponent.

We did this three times, but each time I didn't simply trust that Lincoln was going to beat his opponent: I made sure of it. After what happened against Northwestern, I knew that McIlravy needed a major confidence boost. So as part of my plan, the three Hawkeyes competing in these mock-matches against him knew that, in the end, McIlravy needed to win. All three understood the plan and went along with it. McIlravy never knew.

The only people that knew the predetermined outcomes of these matches were McIlravy's three opponents and myself. The key was that the other wrestlers had to make it look real. In reality, making it look real wasn't a problem, and none of them had to let up to let him win. Their minds and bodies were probably not at their best, knowing they could not win these matches under any circumstances. Still, the important thing for McIlravy and the team was that the plan had worked: in two days, he had three wins in Carver-Hawkeye.

With better confidence, McIlravy battled his opponent from Arizona State into overtime that Sunday and pulled out the victory. He was getting better but still needed more work. With the tough Iowa

State match looming, his determination grew. He was coming back to where I knew he could be.

When he faced his nationally ranked Iowa State opponent, McIlravy won easily. He had his momentum back, and it was the first time he really showed me why I had brought him out of redshirt.

Two weeks later, McIlravy, still not in full force, but improving, captured third place at the Big Ten Tournament. Still, he wasn't exactly where I needed him if we were going to win that third NCAA team championship. Fortunately, going into the NCAAs, we usually break down team practice into individual ones that tie up coaches all day, while the athletes actually spend less time on the mat personally. This again gave us one-on-one time with McIlravy to better prepare him for what was coming up at the national tournament.

McIlravy entered the NCAAs seeded, not very high in his weight class, but seeded just the same. As the tournament progressed from round to round, so did Lincoln's ability to achieve. He told me later that, with each win, his confidence increased. Soon enough, the freshman that had only a month earlier been soundly defeated came face-to-face with the NCAA finals. His opponent would be Gerry Abas of Fresno State.

The finals became a composite of the last month of McIlravy's life. Abas jumped out to a big first period lead and then opened that gap late in the third period. With riding time, the score was actually 13 to 8. In collegiate wrestling, one point for riding time is awarded to wrestlers based on controlling their opponent for one minute or more. This point is tacked on at the end of the match.

Trailing, but making a comeback, McIlravy had to wrestle a near-perfect match to win. When he was taken down again with fifty seconds left, I could see he lost his perfect comeback and what looked like his will to compete. But then, he looked over at the assistant coaches and me, and he could see that we believed he could still win the match. We were still giving him the confidence to win. Lincoln told me later that when he saw us, he thought, "Wow, they still think I can win. . . . That's exactly what I needed then."

With fifty seconds remaining in the national final, McIlravy went to work. He began earning two-point takedowns and immediately giving up one-point escapes to chip away at his opponent's lead. His two-for-one strategy worked, and with the help of a stalling call point and the erasure of riding time against him, the match was one point down. McIlravy then scored a takedown in the match's closing seconds to win and became one of the few true freshmen to win an NCAA wrestling championship.

Looking back now, that was one wild month. It shows, however, that these decisions, as tough as they are, can turn out to be right. It's a good feeling. It helped the team, and it helped my relationship with McIlravy's family.

25

Finishing Strong

The conversation with my father went something like this:

"Dad, everything went great. Everyone is healthy and doing well." I stood in the hospital in Iowa City, just moments after the birth of our fourth child.

On the other end of the receiver was my father, Mack Gable, back home in Waterloo. His voice was anxious as he stumbled over his next question: "Is it a boy or girl?"

"Dad, it's another girl," I said.

Silence. I could practically hear the dead air on the other side of the line.

I was perfectly happy with a girl and had never given much thought to whether I wanted my children to be one sex or another. At that point I had three daughters already, and a fourth was just as exciting and fulfilling as a son would have been. Everyone was healthy, and that was a good thing.

My father, on the other hand, was disappointed. He wanted a grandson, and I knew it. Whatever downward emotion he felt lasted only moments though, especially when I proudly told him the baby's name.

"Dad, we named her Mackenzie. We're going to call her Mackie, after you." I immediately heard a shift in his tone. I could hear his smile and how excited he was that this baby would be named after him.

Mackie is six years younger than her closest sibling, Molly, and she was born into a family that revolved around wrestling. There were never regular holidays like Christmas and Thanksgiving because of the wrestling season, but for our family, the NCAA wrestling tournament was and remains as important a holiday as any other.

"I didn't know anything else for the first ten years of my life," Mackie says about our family today. "I just thought everyone rotated their lives around Iowa Hawkeye wrestling. It was fun! Riding on the chartered buses, going to the matches and tournaments, and being part of the Iowa wrestling program was all I knew. The wrestling was never forced on me or my sisters. It was just what we did. In our family you went and cheered for the Hawkeyes, and you spent spring break at the NCAAs. I remember thinking how odd it was that not every family lived like us. I was so happy during those years."

Then it ended.

When Mackie was ten years old, it wasn't Dan Gable who stepped down from coaching the Hawkeyes, it was her father. Everything she had come to know about her family was suddenly yanked out from under the fifth grader, and with wrestling no longer the center of our home, and her sisters moving on with their personal lives, Mackie was perhaps more confused than anything.

"I didn't understand why my father would take something that was so great away from us," Mackie says. "I only knew my father as a coach. Everything we did was so fun. There were times he would come home from practice mad about something, but I loved my dad being the wrestling coach."

While Mackie didn't understand it at the time, Kathy and I definitely knew the time was right to end my run at Iowa. The sport that

I lived for was slowly killing me, and the only way to save myself was to get out of coaching. I had to get both of my hips replaced, and I was sick all of the time until the season ended. Stepping down when I did was the right thing for me to do, but Mackie was mad about it.

At such a tender age, it was difficult for her to understand why things seemed to be falling apart around her, and she did what many children do when they're dealt a card of insecurity: she rebelled. With me stepping away from coaching and her sisters moving on to college, Mackie became a more difficult child than we were used to. She never did anything to embarrass the family or herself. In fact, Mackie's behavior would be considered normal in many homes, but in our home, where wrestling had always been the compass to steer the ship, a wedge grew between Mackie and me.

"In a lot of ways, I was like every other kid, but probably ten times worse," Mackie says of that time now. "My sisters were doing their thing, and I sort of lost that bond and then we didn't have wrestling, so there were two big gaps in my life."

Mackie became a successful soccer player and filled her life with her friends. When she got to high school, she thought she had fig-ured out how to resolve the emptiness she was experiencing: she decided that wrestling could use another Gable, and that it would be her. This wasn't some passing fancy; she was serious, but her mother and I didn't think it was such a great idea. It would have been co-ed wrestling, so Mackie would have been wrestling boys, and we just weren't comfortable with that. She was disappointed when we told her no, but she accepted it and moved on, focusing on becoming a standout soccer player.

Today she does still wonder what she could have brought to the sport of wrestling, now that women's wrestling is gaining in popu-larity. "I see women my age wrestling, and I sometimes think that could have been me. Most of those women started out wrestling in high school having to wrestle guys. I'm glad to see the sport is available for girls today," she says.

The gap between us remained throughout Mackie's high school years as she chose to stay emotionally detached, even when logic told her to do otherwise. "Having Dad be who he was, one of the best coaches ever, you would have thought that as an athlete I would have taken more advice from him," Mackie says. "Well, I didn't. He would approach me many times to give me advice on whatever sport I was playing, which was mostly soccer, and I would many times give him the cold shoulder. I am actually surprised he would continue to approach me because if I was him, I probably would have given up because of my bad attitude. That is why my dad was such a successful coach. He would never give up on a person. He would frequently ask me if I wanted to be put through a workout, or he would try to give me advice on soccer or just life, and I guess I just never wanted to hear it from him."

Our relationship started to improve when Mackie enrolled at Loras College in Dubuque, Iowa, and played soccer. I could tell Mackie was becoming the little girl who used to follow me around everywhere again. We began to understand each other better.

Mackie met Justin McCord, also a soccer player, while at Loras, and the two married in the summer of 2013. This was also the summer when the future of Olympic wrestling hung in the balance. Mackie, along with our entire family, put on the gloves to save the sport that means so much to our family. One of the pictures from their wedding day includes the entire wedding party wearing white T-shirts that read, "Save Olympic Wrestling."

"Keeping wrestling as an Olympic sport was very important to us as a family," Mackie says. "I think it was even bigger to my sisters because they were already married and had children who were wrestling. That fight was something that pulled our family even closer."

The wedding itself was beautiful. I escorted Mackie down the aisle to the waiting Justin. As I gave my youngest daughter a gentle kiss and took my seat beside Kathy, I knew everything was going to be okay. The smile on Mackie's face spoke volumes. She was so happy to be getting married to Justin. I knew her life was turning out just fine and that Mackie and I were going to continue to improve our relationship. It was a wonderful experience.

26

Mother Knows Best

Shortly after winning the gold at the 1972 Munich Olympics, I was home in Waterloo, Iowa, visiting my parents. As usual, I spent the day across the street at Waterloo West High School working out. Autumn had arrived in Iowa, and the hot summer temperatures had given way to a slight chill. Leaves blew across the street as I walked home, carrying my workout clothes in a gym bag, my stomach grumbling for some food.

When I got home, I opened the door and called out, "I'm home," as I had after wrestling practice hundreds of times before. My mother stood by the kitchen table, watching me. She had seen me come home from wrestling practice all banged up on countless occasions. That particular night, I was as banged up as usual: I had a black eye and was limping. There was nothing extraordinary about it.

When I came in that night though, my mom sat down at the table and looked me in the eye as only a mother can. She simply said, "Dan, it's time to move on."

I had been getting pressure from coaches to keep wrestling competitively, and I was only twenty-three years old, which was pretty young in international wrestling. But my mother had watched as I committed my life solely to wrestling for nearly a decade. Such a lifestyle led to being banged up. Crutches, bandages, neck braces, black eyes, and countless bruises were the norm. Now, I had reached the pinnacle of my sport, of any sport really, and was being hailed an American hero for not just winning the gold, but for doing so by not allowing a single point to be scored on me in the entire Olympic Games as well as beating the Russian handpicked to take me down.

That night, my mom was looking at the pain of a wrestler. It was the same pain she had seen in me for about ten years. When a child hurts, a mother hurts. It's the nature of a mother. My mother knew what was best for me, though, and that night she just knew that it was time to move on.

In reality, my mother is probably the only person who could have made that decision for me. I took her words not as a suggestion, but nearly a direct order from a superior. She made the decision for me, and it was based on her love for me.

So I went from being the man on the mat to being the man prowling the sideline for the Iowa Hawkeyes. I attacked coaching with the same ferocity I had as a wrestler. I sought perfection from my athletes and from myself as a coach. We rarely had the best talent, but we just outworked everyone and attacked our opponents. I ultimately pushed and clawed the Hawkeyes to fifteen NCAA championships.

The beginning of the end of my coaching career came one morning as I got out of bed to start my day. I took one step and my hip just gave out, and I fell into a heap to the bedroom floor. I wound up having to get that hip replaced a month later in January 1997, and then the other hip about a year later. My mother had passed away in 1995, but I knew she was still there and was watching her son suffer again.

Ultimately, coaching was not that much easier on my body than competing had been. I actively wrestled with my younger athletes and continued to get banged up in the Iowa wrestling room. During the long college season, I went in early in the mornings and came home long after sundown.

I lived, like my mother had with me, through the successes and failures of my wrestlers. I always pushed every one of them. I wasn't just there for the guys who were scoring team points all of the time. I was there for and pushing every person in that room.

The Hawkeye matches were starting to take their toll as well. We had to prepare and plan each bout down to the tiniest detail beforehand. At the meets themselves, my explosions of intensity were wearing on me after years of stress. Even after my hip replacement surgeries, the crutches at my side may have slowed me down a step or two, but they in no way interfered with my drive and passion for perfection and victory.

I was just forty-nine when my mother visited me again. It wasn't a vision or anything like that, but it was a visit just the same, the kind only a son could receive from his passed-on mother. Her message to me was the same as the one she gave me that night many years ago at the kitchen table in Waterloo.

"Dan, it's time to get out."

My mother may have passed away, but she could still see what was going on in my life. She saw the beating I was taking, physically and emotionally, and just like before, she knew it was time to move on. She knew it was time to retire from coaching.

Just like before, I obeyed my superior, my mother. She knew it was time and, really, so did I.

EPILOGUE The Patience of Change

The fall of 1966 was an exciting time for the Iowa State Cyclone wrestling program. Coach Harold Nichols's troops had finished second in the NCAA tournament the previous season, and he was now welcoming a highly touted new recruiting class to town. Nichols was putting together a team that would dominate the college wrestling world for the next several years. That new recruiting class included Iowans Dave Martin, Jason Smith, Ed Huffman, Don Gillespie, and myself, as well as Dave Bock from West Virginia and Bill Krum from Montana. We collectively held over fifteen state championships.

In 1966, the NCAA had different rules for athletes than they do today, especially for freshmen, who were not allowed to compete as a part of the team on the varsity level. Instead, they competed "unattached," in open tournaments that did not involve school money or resources. That first year of college was more for adjusting to the rigors of college academics and athletics. It was not a bad idea, but most of those rules are gone now.

The wrestling room at Iowa State was at the top of several flights of stairs. The room itself was full, with two big mats, a drinking fountain, a restroom, and a small storage and office room. The weight room and scale were nearby, along with the lockers, showers, and a steam room we used after practice to recover. The wrestling room did offer a glimpse into the outside world, however, with a two-foot-high window on one wall that overlooked the basketball court. It didn't bring in any sunlight, but it did give us a glimpse of civilization from our uncivilized wrestling room.

Coach Nichols's program consisted of early season training just for the freshmen. While the freshmen trained in the wrestling room, learning a lot of technique and doing live wrestling, the rest of the team was involved in intensive conditioning preparation. They spent a lot of time running outside at a nearby golf course and lifting weights in the weight room, so we didn't see much of them at first. It was a solid month before the two groups combined for the team's first full practice. I had great success wrestling with the other freshmen, even with guys who were bigger than me. This gave me additional confidence about wrestling at the college level, though I was never really lacking in that area. Wrestling was my sport, and my aggressive style was difficult for most to keep up with. I wasn't the most genetically gifted in terms of speed or quickness, but my body type and heavy hips really helped in wrestling. This was my favorite sport, as well as the one I was most dominant in.

When the rest of the team joined us and we practiced together for the first time as a group, I was really looking forward to the challenge. The returning team had several All-Americans and NCAA champions. Among the most notable were Dale Bahr and Vic Marcucci, both national finalists the previous season, and All-American Gary Wallman, a hard-nosed wrestler and also a Golden Gloves boxing champion from South Dakota. Wallman had dominated the prep wrestling scene in his home state, winning titles in each of his high school years before coming to Iowa State.

At one of the first full team practices, Wallman approached me and wanted to wrestle with me for the duration of the practice. I never backed down from a challenge, and this day was no different, even though Wallman wrestled in a lower weight class than I did. Wrestling with him was very different from wrestling with the other freshmen. He was very physical, and even though I battled as hard as I could, we were about even the entire time, with no clear victor. I was upset: even was not good enough for me. That might as well have been a loss. He wasn't even as big as me.

After the two-hour practice, I was covered in sweat, nursing a few mat burns, bumps, and bruises like everyone else, and was shaken by the physical brawl I'd just had with Wallman. As I sat in the haze of the steam room for thirty minutes, I analyzed our bout to figure out what had gone wrong. I wanted to know how Wallman had given me so much trouble. It didn't matter that he was a returning All-American or a Golden Gloves champion; that was not an excuse.

Just a couple of months earlier, I had been training with Bob Buzzard, a fellow native of Waterloo who had just finished a successful wrestling career at Iowa State. Being a high school wrestler getting ready to move there myself, Buzzard felt that I needed to learn a lesson before college. We wrestled on the small mat in my parents' basement. We had trained down there together many times before, but this time he showed me a level of physical intensity that I had never experienced before. When that session with Buzzard was over, I was battered, hurt, and crying, but I also realized that this was my introduction to the next level of wrestling. Having three or four weeks remaining before I left for Ames, I increased my training to be ready for the increased demands. It helped, but I knew more would be needed for continued success in college.

Like the beating Buzzard gave me, my workout with Wallman showed me what I needed to focus on to improve. Buzzard showed me that I had to work harder to keep up in college. With Wallman, I learned that I needed to not just work hard, but I also needed a breakdown of what kind of work I had to do. I had to work both harder *and* smarter. I needed to put more emphasis on techniques and tactics, as well as continue to physically train harder.

I had discovered a way to turn disappointment and frustration into success and victory. I would improve by training both harder and smarter. I took stock of my strengths and areas that needed improvement as a wrestler and used that increased awareness to put together a plan to get more physical. I then committed myself to that plan, which included heavier weight lifting, rope climbing, more running, increased drilling, and wrestling even harder.

Much of my plan for physical improvement, as it did then and does today, had to do with a thirty-day philosophy. When you want to make a change in any area of your life, you have to make a decision as to what you are going to do differently in order to make that change. Then you stay on that path for thirty days. Those thirty days then turn into sixty days, and so forth. The reason most people fail to make changes in any area of their life is because they often say, "I made the change," and then are frustrated when they don't notice an immediate difference the next day or in two days. It doesn't happen like that. I was not the first person to implement this philosophy, but even at eighteen, I knew that thirty days of consistent focus and work would lead to long-term change and success.

Sitting in the steam room that day at Iowa State, I recommitted myself to being the best wrestler possible. I knew that I was not going to let Wallman wrestle even with me again. I also knew that it would take a tremendous amount of work to be able to dominate a great wrestler like him. So I ratcheted up my training. I got to training earlier and remained later. I sacrificed social activities and downtime, all because I was upset and angry that Wallman had wrestled even with me. This was my focus each day, and I arose with the resolve to be the hardest, smartest, and most physical worker on the Iowa State team.

About a month later, I saw the fruits of my wrestling labors. Wallman challenged me to wrestle in practice again, and I was ready. My focus was like a laser as I went after Wallman with everything I had. I was not going to be deadlocked this time. No, I was going to send a message to the entire team that I was working to be the best in that room and beyond. On that wintry day in the wrestling room at Iowa State, this time it was one-sided. My side.

■ ■ ■

When I was the coach at the University of Iowa, wrestlers came in from all across the country for summer camps with the Hawkeyes.

This always gave me another opportunity to see how this thirty-day philosophy can come to fruition. I told the athletes that the camp was going to be brutal and intense, but whether they were at one of the twelve-day camps or the twenty-one-day camps, if they stayed focused, they would enjoy a great change.

For the wrestlers who kept their game face on for the duration of the camp, there usually came a point where they could feel the positive changes. Sometimes it happened on the ninth day, sometimes the tenth, sometimes even later, but it happened for almost every young man who came to these camps and remained focused on the plan we set out for them. They could feel the change, but it didn't happen overnight and it didn't happen without a lot of effort.

To this day, I don't believe it when people tell me that they have tried something that will help them make some kind of change and complain that it didn't work. If you stick to the proven formula of doing something for thirty days and believe in it and in yourself, a change will happen. But you have to stick to it. I have seen this plan succeed in too many people, including myself, to discount it.

In addition to the thirty-day philosophy, I also believe that another step toward creating success comes through the ten thousand hours philosophy. In his 2008 book, *Outliers: The Story of Success*, Malcolm Gladwell explains that, based on current research, in order for success and change to occur, one must work toward that change for ten thousand hours. Thirty years before Gladwell wrote this book, I had already proven this.

Before I ever wrestled a college match my sophomore year, I had trained for ten thousand hours. It wasn't always fun, and it was hard work, but it takes hard work to make changes in your life. Anything worthwhile is going to require work. And how long do we work at something we want to change? As long as it takes.

I followed this ten thousand hours philosophy as a college wrestler, and it paid off. In matches and practice sessions, my extra work led to me separating from the rest of the pack. I kept getting better and better, even at this higher level of competition. It took that original thirty-day commitment on my part to get started and actually start to see the changes, and then the ten thousand hour accumulation to fully bring it about.

As I started to dominate in the Iowa State wrestling room, I put together a game with those willing to take me up on a challenge. I would spot almost anyone twenty points. When the first three minutes of wrestling began, I just attacked and attacked and attacked. Every time I did this, the results were the same: I outscored those twenty points . . . in the first period. It was that kind of constant intensity that helped keep me sharp and striving for perfection.

But one of the most important ways I have always improved is through trials or defeat. It was wrestling to a draw against Wallman in practice that put me on the path to dominate the Iowa State wrestling room with the thirty-day mindset. One of the greatest changes and improvements in my life was born out of my greatest athletic disappointment. I won 181 consecutive high school and college matches before losing to Larry Owings in the 1970 NCAA finals. It was after that loss that I got really good. I improved more in the one year following my defeat to Owings than I did in the seven years prior, when I was undefeated.

What's important is staying patient and remaining focused while knowing that you will hit those new levels of success in time. Analyzing what needs to be changed makes a big difference in future outcomes. Even when you get to the point where you are among the very best in wrestling, or whatever it is you do, there can still be improvement. If you are able to stay the course, you can continue to separate and pull ahead of the rest of the pack. You won't always know when that change will happen, but if you remain patient, it will. Remember, don't wait for it to happen. Make it happen, as soon as possible, by great preparation.

■ ■ ■

The patience of change was once forced on me by an injury as well. In the middle of February 1972, practice was over in the Iowa State wrestling room when the smallest wrestler on the team, Norm Wilkerson, grabbed me and wanted to try to take me down. I laughed, knowing that even Chris Taylor, the biggest wrestler in the room, had a difficult time doing so. With that in mind, I let Wilkerson start from any position he wanted. I was extremely confident of winning from any position, and I didn't expect it to last long. It didn't. Within seconds, I was lying on the mat with my knee in extreme pain.

To make matters worse, I was supposed to fly to Lehigh University the next day to wrestle in a dual match with the Soviet Union's team. At that time, I was the current world champion, so I was the match's headliner. That night, I lay in bed waiting for the injury to go away. It didn't, and I ended up having to call the match organizers to let them know I would not be able to compete. I had never missed a match in my nine years of wrestling since high school. I wept.

One thousand miles away at Lehigh University, when the Russians heard that I would not be competing, my opponent reportedly shouted for joy: "No Gable! No Gable!" They sent my intended opponent to wrestle Wayne Wells instead, who was in the next higher weight class. The Russian lost anyway, as Wells was the 1970 world champion in the 163-pound weight class.

The knee injury did not go away quickly though, so I went to see a specialist. They told me that the knee was going to need surgery, which would have put me out of the Olympics. I told them no, not now. I needed help though, so I went back to the man who put me on the path to becoming a dominant wrestler: my high school wrestling coach and guidance counselor, Coach Bob Siddens. Fortunately, he had an answer that did not involve surgery: a good dog bone tape job, which really did help.

Three or four days after the initial injury, my knee was starting to feel better and the tape job made me feel stronger so that I could practice again. I couldn't shoot, but at least I could stand there and counter. This wasn't enough though, so I started to adopt a new way of wrestling, scoring off opponents' actions and learning to force them to create action.

This wasn't just a defensive style, as I had to learn hand fighting and control ties to better set up my opponent so I could score without getting hurt further. The knee tap, a move Bobby Douglas showed me after the Olympic Trials in 1968, surfaced over and over again from this position, and I eventually used it to score more times than I can remember. In reality, I should have adopted this move earlier, rather than being forced to because of an injury.

This injury may have temporarily shut down my aggressive style, but this adaptation of an entirely different way to score off of defense was ultimately very useful. Before it was just offense, offense, offense. Now it was a more defensive-offensive way of scoring. This patience of change took about two months to master, but as my knee got stronger, I was able to go back to my original style of wrestling more, and mix the two styles up. It's where I coined the phrase, "I shoot, I score. You shoot, I score."

That injury actually made me a better wrestler, but I could have learned these tactics under normal circumstances. I just wish I hadn't waited until extreme circumstances forced me to.

Dan Gable Achievements, Stats, & Life Record

1959   **State of Iowa YMCA backstroke swimming champion**, age 11, Waterloo, Iowa

1964   **State of Iowa wrestling champion**, Waterloo West High School

1965   **State of Iowa wrestling champion**, Waterloo West High School

1966   **State of Iowa wrestling champion**, Outstanding Athlete in All Sports, Waterloo West High School

1966   **Midlands Tournament champion**, Iowa State University

1967   **Midlands Tournament champion**, Iowa State University

1968   **Big Eight champion**, Iowa State University
NCAA national champion, Iowa State University
Midlands Tournament champion, Iowa State University

1969   **Big Eight champion**, Iowa State University
NCAA national champion, Iowa State University
Outstanding Wrestler in NCAA Award, Iowa State University
Gorriaran Award for most pins in least amount of time at NCAA, Iowa State University
US Freestyle national champion, wrestling unattached
Midlands Tournament champion, Iowa State University

1970   **Big Eight champion**, Iowa State University
NCAA runner-up, Iowa State University
Gorriaran Award for most pins in least amount of time at NCAA, Iowa State University
US Freestyle national champion, wrestling unattached
Midlands Tournament champion, Iowa State University

1971   **Pan-American Games champion**, Cali, Columbia
US Freestyle national champion, wrestling unattached
World Freestyle champion, Sofia, Bulgaria
Midlands Tournament champion, Iowa State University

1972   **Tblisi Tournament champion**, Tblisi, USSR
Outstanding Wrestler, Tblisi, USSR
Olympic gold medalist, Munich, West Germany

1980 **Head coach** of the US Olympic Freestyle Wrestling Team

1984 **Head coach** of the US Olympic Freestyle Wrestling team

2000 **Head coach** of the US Olympic Freestyle Wrestling Team

INDIVIDUAL ATHLETIC STATS

1964–1970, 181 consecutive wins (117 consecutive wins in college / 64 consecutive wins in high school)

Consecutive pins during college, 34 (24 NCAA recognized matches + 10 additional at two outside tournaments)

Iowa State University record in pins, 85

1972 Munich Olympics, 6 matches at Olympics (+15 others to make United States team, 21 matches total)

1972 US Olympic Trials, 9 pins and 6 decisions (totaling 101–1 points scored)

1972 Olympics, 3 pins and 3 decisions on opponent (totaling 29–0 points scored)

National Freestyle wrestling record, 67 wins, 5 losses, and 1 tie

International Freestyle record, 32 wins, 1 loss, and 1 tie

Overall Freestyle record, 99 wins, 6 losses, and 2 ties (4 of those losses occurred in freshmen and sophomore years of college)

COACHING STATS, 1977–1997

21-Year Total Record, 355 wins, 21 losses, and 5 ties

NCAA Team Titles, 15

All-Americans, 152

NCAA Points, 2536.75

Big Ten Duals, 131 wins, 2 losses, and 1 tie

National Champions, 45

NCAA Finalists, 78

Big Ten Champions, 106

Big Ten Championships, 21

At Carver-Hawkeye Arena, Duals 98–1, 1983 Big Tens 1st place, 1986 NCAAs 1st place, 1991 NCAAs 1st place, 1994 Big Tens 1st place, 1995 NCAAs 1st place

OVERALL LIFE RECORD

Sister Diane's death, 1964. **Loss.**

Loss to Larry Owings in final NCAA match, 1970. **Loss.**

World Championship, 1971. **Win.**

Olympic gold medal, unscored upon, 1972. **Win.**

Lost what would have been Iowa's tenth consecutive NCAA
Championship, 1987. **Loss.**

Retired with a record team performance, 15 NCAA Championships and
21 straight Big Ten Championships, 1997. **Win.**

My family. It has grown from 4 people to 20 people (and is still
growing!), and all are happy and healthy, present day. **Win.**

I'm still ahead, **4 to 3**.

Teammates & Teams Coached

1959, Waterloo YMCA Swim Team, Waterloo, Iowa
Teammates: Rick Young, John Pederson, John Walker, Tom Penaluna, Bill Tate, Vic Laughlin, Greg Apel
Coaches: Wally Lessman, Chuck Hazama

1964, Waterloo West High School, team took second place in state
State Teammates: Dale Anderson*, Ed Heene*, Bud Knox, Wally Markham, Larry Orvis
Coaches: Head Coach Bob Siddens, Assistant Coach Dick Walker

1965, Waterloo West High School, team took first place in state
State Teammates: Phil Sherburne, Dan Mashek, Bruce McClintock, Bud Knox*
Coaches: Head Coach Bob Siddens, Assistant Coach Dick Walker

1966, Waterloo West High School, team took first place in state
State Teammates: Marty Dickey*, Phil Sherburne*, Bob Heene, Mike Cowell
Coaches: Head Coach Bob Siddens, Assistant Coach Bill Blake

1968, Iowa State University, team took second place at NCAA
All-Americans: Gary Wallman, Dale Bahr*, Reg Wicks*, Jason Smith
Big Eight Champions: Mike Schmauss, Jim Duschen

1969, Iowa State University, team took first place at NCAA
All-Americans: Steve Lampe, Mike Schmauss, Carl Adams, Dave Martin*, Jason Smith*, Chuck Jean*, Jim Duschen, Wayne Beske
Big Eight Champions: Jim Duschen

* = State or NCAA Champion

1970, Iowa State University, team took first place at NCAA

All-Americans: Phil Parker, Dave Martin*, Jason Smith*, Chuck Jean*, Ben Peterson

Big Eight Champions: Phil Parker, Carl Adams, Jason Smith, Ben Peterson

1971, World Championships, Sofia, Bulgaria, United States team took fourth place

Medalists: Don Behm, silver; Russ Hellickson, bronze

1973, Assistant Coach under Head Coach Gary Kurdelmeier, University of Iowa, team took seventh place in the NCAA and second place in the Big Ten

1974, Assistant Coach under Head Coach Gary Kurdelmeier, University of Iowa, team took fifth place in the NCAA and first place in the Big Ten

1975, Assistant Coach under Head Coach Gary Kurdelmeier, University of Iowa, team took first place in the NCAA (University of Iowa's first national title in any sport) and first place in the Big Ten

1976, Assistant Coach under Head Coach Gary Kurdelmeier, University of Iowa, team took first place in the NCAA and first place in the Big Ten

1977, Head Coach, University of Iowa, team took third place in the NCAA and first place in the Big Ten

All-Americans: John Bowlsby, Chris Campbell*, Mike DeAnna, Mike McGivern, Keith Mourlam

Big Ten Champions: John Bowlsby, Chris Campbell, Mike DeAnna, Steve Hunte, Keith Mourlam

1978, Head Coach, University of Iowa, team took first place in the NCAA and first place in the Big Ten

* = State or NCAA Champion

All-Americans: John Bowlsby, Mike DeAnna, Dan Glenn, Bruce Kinseth, Randy Lewis, Scott Trizzino

Big Ten Champions: John Bowlsby, Mike DeAnna, Dan Glenn, Steve Hunte, Randy Lewis, Greg Stevens

1979, Head Coach, University of Iowa, team took first place in the NCAA and first place in the Big Ten

All-Americans: Mike DeAnna, Dan Glenn, Bruce Kinseth*, Randy Lewis*, Bud Palmer, Scott Trizzino

Big Ten Champions: Mike DeAnna, Dan Glenn, Bruce Kinseth, Randy Lewis, Bud Palmer, Scott Trizzino

1980, Head Coach, University of Iowa, team took first place in the NCAA and first place in the Big Ten

All-Americans: Doug Anderson, Ed Banach*, Dan Glenn, Randy Lewis*, King Mueller, Dean Phinney, Mark Stevenson, Lennie Zalesky

Big Ten Champions: Ed Banach, Dan Glenn, Randy Lewis, Lennie Zalesky

1981, Head Coach, University of Iowa, team took first place in the NCAA and first place in the Big Ten

All-Americans: Ed Banach*, Lou Banach*, Barry Davis, Mike DeAnna, Randy Lewis, Tim Riley, Scott Trizzino, Jim Zalesky, Lennie Zalesky

Big Ten Champions: Ed Banach, Lou Banach, Pete Bush, Barry Davis, Mike DeAnna, Scott Trizzino, Lennie Zalesky

1982, Head Coach, University of Iowa, team took first place in the NCAA and first place in the Big Ten

All-Americans: Ed Banach, Lou Banach, Pete Bush*, Barry Davis*, Dave Fitzgerald, Jeff Kerber, Jim Zalesky*, Lennie Zalesky

Big Ten Champions: Ed Banach, Pete Bush, Barry Davis, Jeff Kerber, Mark Trizzino, Jim Zalesky, Lennie Zalesky

1983, Head Coach, University of Iowa, team took first place in the NCAA and first place in the Big Ten

* = State or NCAA Champion

147

All-Americans: Ed Banach*, Lou Banach*, Barry Davis*, Duane
Goldman, Jim Heffernan, Jeff Kerber, Harlan Kistler, Tim Riley,
Jim Zalesky*

Big Ten Champions: Ed Banach, Lou Banach, Barry Davis, Duane
Goldman, Jim Heffernan, Jeff Kerber, Harlan Kistler, Tim Riley,
Jim Zalesky

1984, Head Coach, University of Iowa, team took first place in the
NCAA and first place in the Big Ten

All-Americans: Duane Goldman, Jeff Kerber, Lindley Kistler, Marty
Kistler, Greg Randall, Tim Riley, Mark Trizzino, Jim Zalesky*

Big Ten Champions: Pete Bush, Duane Goldman, Jeff Kerber, Lindley
Kistler, Marty Kistler, Greg Randall, Jim Zalesky

1985, Head Coach, University of Iowa, team took first place in the
NCAA and first place in the Big Ten

All-Americans: Barry Davis*, Rico Chiapparelli, Kevin Dresser, Matt
Egeland, Duane Goldman, Jim Heffernan, Lindley Kistler, Marty
Kistler*, Greg Randall

Big Ten Champions: Rico Chiapparelli, Barry Davis, Kevin Dresser, Matt
Egeland, Duane Goldman, Jim Heffernan, Lindley Kistler, Marty Kistler

1986, Head Coach, University of Iowa, team took first place in the
NCAA and first place in the Big Ten

All-Americans: Royce Alger, Rico Chiapparelli, Kevin Dresser*, Duane
Goldman*, Jim Heffernan*, Marty Kistler*, Brad Penrith*, Greg Randall

Big Ten Champions: Royce Alger, Rico Chiapparelli, Kevin Dresser,
Duane Goldman, Jim Heffernan, Marty Kistler, Brad Penrith

1987, Head Coach, University of Iowa, team took second place in the
NCAA and first place in the Big Ten

All-Americans: Royce Alger*, Rico Chiapparelli*, Jim Heffernan, John
Heffernan, Brad Penrith, Mark Sindlinger

* = State or NCAA Champion

Big Ten Champions: Royce Alger, Rico Chiapparelli, Jim Heffernan, Brad Penrith, John Regan, Mark Sindlinger

1988, Head Coach, University of Iowa, team took second place in the NCAA and first place in the Big Ten
All-Americans: Royce Alger*, John Heffernan, Joe Melchiore, Brad Penrith, Mark Sindlinger
Big Ten Champions: Royce Alger, John Heffernan, Brad Penrith, Mark Sindlinger

1989, Head Coach, University of Iowa, team took sixth place in the NCAA and first place in the Big Ten
All-Americans: Tom Brands, Steve Martin, Joe Melchiore, Mark Reiland
Big Ten Champions: Tom Brands

1990, Head Coach, University of Iowa, team took third place in the NCAA and first place in the Big Ten
All-Americans: Terry Brands*, Tom Brands*, Bart Chelesvig, Brooks Simpson, Troy Steiner, Doug Streicher
Big Ten Champions: Terry Brands, Brooks Simpson

1991, Head Coach, University of Iowa, team took first place in the NCAA and first place in the Big Ten
All-Americans: Terry Brands, Tom Brands*, Bart Chelesvig, Travis Fiser, Mark Reiland*, Tom Ryan, Terry Steiner, Troy Steiner, Chad Zaputil
Big Ten Champions: Terry Brands, Tom Brands, Tom Ryan, Troy Steiner, Chad Zaputil

1992, Head Coach, University of Iowa, team took first place in the NCAA and first place in the Big Ten
All-Americans: Terry Brands*, Tom Brands*, Bart Chelesvig, Travis Fiser, John Oostendorp, Tom Ryan, Terry Steiner, Troy Steiner*, Chad Zaputil

* = State or NCAA Champion

Big Ten Champions: Terry Brands, Tom Brands, John Oostendorp, Tom Ryan, Troy Steiner, Chad Zaputil

1993, Head Coach, University of Iowa, team took first place in the NCAA and first place in the Big Ten

All-Americans: Ray Brinzer, Lincoln McIlravy*, John Oostendorp, Joel Sharratt, Terry Steiner*, Troy Steiner, Chad Zaputil

Big Ten Champions: Troy Steiner, Chad Zaputil

1994, Head Coach, University of Iowa, team took second place in the NCAA and first place in the Big Ten

All-Americans: Lincoln McIlravy*, Jeff McGinness, Mike Mena, Joel Sharratt*, Daryl Weber, Joe Williams

Big Ten Champions: Ray Brinzer, Lincoln McIlravy

1995, Head Coach, University of Iowa, team took first place in the NCAA and first place in the Big Ten

All-Americans: Ray Brinzer, Mark Ironside, Jeff McGinness*, Lincoln McIlravy, Mike Mena, Matt Nerem, Joel Sharratt, Daryl Weber, Bill Zadick

Big Ten Champions: Ray Brinzer, Mark Ironside, Jeff McGinness, Lincoln McIlravy, Mike Mena, Joel Sharratt

1996, Head Coach, University of Iowa, team took first place in the NCAA and first place in the Big Ten

All-Americans: Lee Fullhart, Mike Mena, Mark Ironside, Mike Uker, Joe Williams*, Daryl Weber*, Bill Zadick*

Big Ten Champions: Mark Ironside, Daryl Weber, Joe Williams, Bill Zadick

1997, Head Coach, University of Iowa, team took first place in the NCAA and first place in the Big Ten

All-Americans: Lee Fullhart*, Kasey Gilliss, Mark Ironside*, Lincoln McIlravy*, Mike Mena, Mike Uker, Jessie Whitmer*, Joe Williams*

Big Ten Champions: Mark Ironside, Lincoln McIlravy

* = State or NCAA Champion

Index